# Contents

# Preface

This professional development package (which includes this INSET manual and the handbook which accompanies it), is the culmination of two years' work by a group of teachers, advisers and other education workers who were brought together by the ASE as their "Multicultural Education Working Party". The original brief for the group was to prepare a draft policy statement for the ASE. The Working Party soon realised, however, that there was a great need and demand from many teachers in all phases of education for more than just a policy! They wanted training materials, classroom resources and, above all, the opportunity to discuss the issues and share perspectives and practice.

So the group, supported by the ASE, expanded its brief and developed a number of projects. The first was to produce a discussion paper which would provide teachers with a concise, yet comprehensive overview of the issues of science, equality and anti-racism in education. This document, which went through extensive consultation within the ASE and 'outside', formed the overall framework for the group's work and it gives our collective viewpoint on the issues. It is published here as an appendix to the manual and forms an important reference point for all the workshops. Meanwhile, the Working Party also organised events at the ASE Annual Meetings in 1990 and 1991, including symposia, discussion groups and displays which were very well received and were attended by large numbers of teachers. Training materials used at these and other sessions form the basis of several of the workshops in this pack – and have been extensively reviewed in the light of the comments from colleagues.

The final stage of our new brief was to prepare this package of materials for publication. We were aware that other colleagues had been working in this field for many years in projects based in London, Birmingham Leicestershire and elsewhere, and we were anxious to build on a full range of good practice in what we came to term "science for equality and justice". Several colleagues outside the group were, therefore, invited to contribute to the project – both as writers of INSET materials and of chapters and articles for the handbook. The result is, we feel, an exciting and innovative package, firmly based in classroom practice and reflecting developments in all phases and areas, and one which never loses sight of the commitment, shared by us all, to a science curriculum which is anti-racist in its contexts, processes and content, and which provides for equality of access and achievement for all pupils and students in the multicultural society of the 1990s.

And, by the way, we did produce a policy!

**Kabir Shaikh: Chair – ASE Multicultural Education Working Party.**

**Steve Thorp: Editor**

An active INSET manual
for teachers and educators

# RACE, EQUALITY AND SCIENCE TEACHING

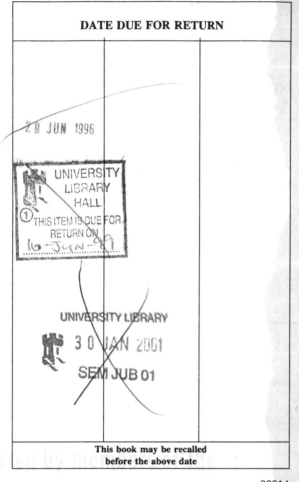
Wri
ASE
Working Party

Edited by Steve Thorp

Produced for ASE by Fieldwork Ltd

Published by the Association for
Science Education 1991

© ASE 1991

Printed by The Lavenham Press

ISBN 0 86357 165 4

Publication supported by ASE/BP Fellowship 1991

# Introduction

This active INSET manual is designed to be used with teachers to address the issues of "race, equality and science teaching" in all phases of education. A rationale and theoretical framework for the materials is provided in the discussion paper (Appendix 1) and, in more detail, in the handbook which accompanies this manual. The introduction to the discussion paper states:

"The Working Party believes that issues of racism and access to the curriculum for all children in a multicultural society need to be addressed as a matter of urgency".

The Working Party also emphasises the:

"potential of science to enhance the curriculum by drawing on the richness and diversity of cultures and on the practice of science, now and throughout history ...(and) the powerful role of science teaching for combatting racism and prejudice in society".

In order to address the issues above, the focus of the manual is firmly on the classroom and curriculum. That is not to diminish the continuing importance of teachers challenging racism in the wider community (quite the opposite), but rather to put the emphasis on what teachers can do best to challenge racism – that is to teach! By developing the understanding and skills to address these complex and often sensitive issues with students and colleagues, teachers may then feel more confident in working for equality and justice in the classroom alongside struggles against inequality and injustice in their communities, society and the world.

This focus on classroom and school requires an approach to the science curriculum which can help prepare all our young people for, in the words of the Working Party:

"• life in our culturally diverse society in which there is systematic discrimination directed against some of its groups;
• an awareness of the complex relationships and inequalities between and within nations;
• the increasing interdependance between peoples in the world.

All this will involve addressing the nature and contexts of science and racism at all levels in education and devising strategies for providing genuine access to science for children from all groups in our society".

Although this manual is specifically concerned with "Race, Equality and Science Education", we recognise that this is only one dimension in the struggle for equality and justice – alongside gender and class – and this work will have implications for the education of working class pupils, girls and those with special needs and different physical abilities. The manual should also be seen in the wider context of recent developments in the science curriculum and education legislation. For example, we endorse and welcome more systematic approaches to curriculum and policy development – with equality issues it is essential that 'policy is put into practice' and that success or failure can be evaluated in an objective and positive way.

We also recognise that the Education Reform Act continues to dominate the agenda of many teachers in many parts of the country, but we believe that some recent developments are unlikely to promote equality; indeed some legislation has been specifically designed to work against such moves. In the manual, and the handbook accompanying it, we acknowledge the importance of these recent developments whilst also concerning ourselves with a wider and longer term agenda than that provided by the ERA and the present National Curriculum. Whilst one workshop is entitled "National Curriculum" and is intended to help teachers map equality issues in their curricular planning, the manual wishes to avoid a narrow focus on England and Wales. We hope it will be of much wider use and help teachers address issues and concerns which transcend these narrow, contemporary political frameworks, whilst realising the agendas that many teachers will currently be working to. We hope that we have achieved a realistic balance!

The manual is designed to provide teachers and others concerned with science education with the relevant skills and understanding to deal with equality and justice issues positively and effectively in their classrooms and institutions. It includes support in curriculum planning, devising relevant contexts, dealing with racism and developing, implementing and reviewing policy. Teachers should, however, feel free to use the manual as a flexible resource and not feel that the full 'course' should be followed. It should be used alongside the articles, perspectives and exemplars contained in the handbook, and the whole package will, we hope, be a 'tool' for equality for all those teaching science into the 1990s and beyond.

**Steve Thorp: November 1991**

# The manual

The manual is designed to be used flexibly by groups of teachers in school staff meetings, science departments, or at INSET course sessions. It has been developed as a comprehensive and self-contained 'course' which could be worked through section by section. However, it is designed for more flexible use and many of the sections and workshops are appropriate for use as shorter courses or for insertion into training packages. If the manual is used in this way, however, we would recommend that, as a minimum, the "Discussion paper" (appendix 1) is provided as a handout to ensure that the theoretical position underpinning the materials is made clear.

It contains 21 inter-active workshops divided into four sections as shown on the "Pack framework" diagram. The "Initial reflections" and "Starters" sections are intended as introductory workshops to prepare the ground for more in-depth activities. "Curriculum issues" is the central section containing a range of workshops addressing issues of process and practice, context and content. The final section provides a systematic and active model for "Policy development and review" which can be easily adapted as a whole-school planning tool, regardless of a science focus. Each section has brief introductory notes which include suggestions for using the workshops and a list of all the workshops with brief descriptors. The workshops themselves are clearly set out and all supporting materials are provided. The support materials themselves are varied and stimulating, and include a range of realistic contexts, scenarios, classroom materials and viewpoints. The sections are:

## INITIAL REFLECTIONS
Two workshops based on checklist activities, which enable teachers to establish their own starting points as individuals or teams with relation to a range of practice and policy issues;

## STARTERS
Three workshops which set the context and parameters of the pack and which explore teachers' views of the nature of science, science education and culture within a theoretical framework of 'equality and justice';

## CURRICULUM ISSUES
Eleven in-depth workshops which address various curriculum practice issues. There are three 'core' units which build on the previous two sections by further developing awareness and analysis, and enable teachers and facilitators to plan further training flexibly. Eight 'foundation' workshops deal with various processes and contexts promoting equality and justice;

## POLICY DEVELOPMENT AND REVIEW
Five workshops which provide a systematic model for developing and implementing policy through the stages of deciding which issues to address, consultation, writing policy statements, devising action plans and developing monitoring procedures and success criteria.

# Using the workshops

All the workshops are written with the assumption that sessions will be organised and run by a workshop coordinator or facilitator. However the materials can easily be adapted for use by teams or small groups of teachers who wish to work through the pack collectively. The key to success for both methods of use is good preparation – which will include thorough reading of all notes, copying relevant support materials and making sure handouts are available. The facilitator's role in more formal training is crucial and will include leading plenary discussions, as well as setting up group activities in a way which builds on the experience and meets the training needs of participants. However, the supporting material provided in the manual (and handbook) is designed to enable facilitators to do this with confidence.

Each workshop is set out in an easy to follow, consistent format which includes the following headings.

## PURPOSE

Setting out the aims of the session and what the workshop hopes to achieve. In evaluation, participants should be asked to refer back to the 'purpose' to assess effectiveness.

## RESOURCES

This sets out briefly what is needed to run the workshop. It includes specific page references for support materials and handouts required, as well as more basic requirements. As a rule of thumb, facilitators can assume that for every workshop a supply of A4 paper, large and small fibre pens, large A2 paper and/or flipchart/writing board will be required. For many, an O.H.P. and blank acetates will also be useful. Facilitators should read the workshop notes thoroughly and prepare appropriate numbers of copies of support materials prior to the workshop.

## TIME

The total time required for the workshop; this is an estimate only and facilitators should use their own discretion on timings.

## PROCEDURE

This is a more detailed description of the workshop, with instructions for facilitators to follow. They include detailed timings, descriptions of how materials are to be used and give advice on group sizes, ways of recording and reporting back, etc. In some workshops specific scenarios and/or tasks may be described; in others the activities are simply listed. This will often depend on the nature of the supporting materials. Although the "Procedure" is what the facilitator will follow most closely during the workshop, detailed reference should have been made, prior to the workshop, to the "Notes for facilitators".

Most workshops will involve a number of standard processes using a variety of stimuli and support materials.

## SMALL GROUP WORK

Unless otherwise stated, small group work usually means three or four participants. Pair work will also sometimes be specified. The range of tasks will include: brainstorming (i.e., generating lists of ideas); sorting and prioritising exercises on lists, ideas, statement cards, etc.; discussing scenarios; structured role play; discussing an issue. On most occasions participants will be asked to make brief notes for reporting back to the main group. It is often useful to ask groups to nominate a 'reporter' to ensure that reports are clear and concise. The kind of tasks and activities are varied throughout the pack to ensure a range of small group strategies. Unless stated, it is strongly recommended that the facilitator does not intervene in small group activities and discussion. The purpose of such sessions is for participants to draw out and explore their collective viewpoints, not for the facilitator to give their view. One exception to this may be when a facilitator is asked to clarify processes, activities or materials provided, although good preparation and clear introduction of tasks should eliminate the need for this in most cases.

## PLENARY SESSIONS

Whole group or plenary sessions are often invaluable at the beginning and end of a workshop or workshop stage. They are particularly useful for staged workshops where groups are required to sum up certain points before moving onto the next issue or activity. In general they will consist of one, or both, of the following processes:

1 Reporting back is a regular activity whereby participants share their views and discussions with others. If groups have all been considering one issue, then the report back will highlight differing points of view and perspectives. This is particularly useful in stimulating whole group discussion where teachers can feel confident in expressing their views. If groups have been considering different issues or aspects of an issue, the report back becomes a 'jigsaw' session whereby the groups' pieces contribute to a whole group understanding of an issue.

**2** Group discussion will usually be introduced by the facilitator, often following a report back session, or by presenting a brief talk based on a handout or O.H.P. slide. Stimulus 'discussion' questions will often be suggested and participants should be encouraged to respond to them. Here the facilitator's style will be interventionist, and they may be required to add certain points that the group has not raised or dealt with in enough depth. Good preparation, background knowledge and an awareness of the issue being discussed are important.

### INDIVIDUAL REFLECTION

This is most likely to occur at the beginning and/or end of a workshop. Participants may be asked, at the beginning, to write down a sentence or two describing their current viewpoint on a particular issue using a stimulus question provided. This can then be kept as a reference point throughout the workshop and reviewed at the end. At the end of a workshop, reflection is most likely to come as part of the evaluation stage, although a few workshops have additional reflection activities built in which supplement the standard evaluation format.

### EVALUATION

It is important that evaluation takes place after each workshop in order to:

• assess how effective the workshop has been in meeting the needs of participants and addressing the stated purpose;

• aid planning for future training in this area.

Facilitators may, of course, have their own evaluation processes and these can be adapted for any of the workshops. In some workshops, participants are asked to review their original 'reflections' at the end, and this may serve as an evaluation process itself. A more detailed guide to evaluating the processes and content of the workshops is contained in Appendix 3 of the manual, together with a simple evaluation sheet which facilitators can adapt for use.

### NOTES FOR FACILITATORS

This is probably the most important part of each workshop and facilitators are urged to read these notes carefully in conjunction with the other parts above. The notes will be less structured in nature than the 'procedure'. They are designed to:

• provide facilitators with more detailed guidance and 'hints' on how to run particular activities well and the preparation required. Additional optional or alternative activities may also be suggested here;

• highlight issues which should, or may, emerge during discussion, and provide guidance on what issues the facilitator should raise, and how to raise them;

• provide reference points within the support materials and appendices.

### SUPPORTING MATERIALS

These pages will include all the additional materials that are needed to run workshops and will be found, in a block, at the end of each section. Materials required will be clearly referenced in the workshops for easy access. Much of the material is based on classroom or school scenarios which have been carefully written to reflect actual practice – often being adapted from real incidents or situations.

Typical materials include:

• **Task sheets:** usually containing task descriptions and information for group discussion. One sheet needs to be copied and cut for each group;

• **Statement sheets:** usually containing a range of viewpoints on a particular issue to stimulate discussion. They require copying and cutting – usually one set per group;

• **Context or scenario sheets:** usually describing realistic classroom or school scenarios which require groups to discuss or role play responses. They require copying and cutting as above;

• **Classroom activities:** usually provided to illustrate a process or context issue which will be developed further in discussion. Usually one set per group needs copying, but participants may wish to have these as handouts;

• **Planning models and grids:** usually providing a framework for planning or discussing a curriculum or policy issue. Can often be adapted for use in actual planning. One set per group required for exercise, plus blanks for handouts;

• **Handout sheets:** usually giving some background written or diagrammatic information and definitions to support and/or be used as reference material in the workshop activities. One set per participant required;

• **O.H.P. Originals:** usually included for facilitator to use either as task descriptions, or as a summary of background information required for the workshop. One set per workshop usually requires preparation.

Other materials for specific workshops include photographs, transcripts for taping, etc. Facilitators need to be familiar with these and with any further materials required.

**Note:** unless the facilitator is experienced at leading role play, simulation or other drama activities, it may be useful to consult a colleague who has such experience or expertise. Refer also to the notes on running role play and simulation which appear on pages 152 and 153.

# An active **INSET** manual: workshop guide

## STARTERS

**Issues in science, education and Society**

### WORKSHOPS

- What is science?
- What is culture?
- What is science education for?

## INITIAL REFLECTIONS

**Reviewing existing practice**

### WORKSHOPS

- Looking at my classroom
- Looking at our school/college

## CURRICULUM ISSUES

**Curriculum content, contexts and processes in science education**

### 'CORE' WORKSHOPS

- Science for people
- Principles into practice
- Race and racism

### 'FOUNDATION' WORKSHOPS

#### 'Processes'

- Teaching and learning for equality
- Assessment
- Language and learning
- Groupings in the classroom

#### 'Contexts'

- Images in science
- Science themes
- Science systems
- National Curriculum

## POLICY DEVELOPMENT AND REVIEW

**Processes for writing and implementing policy**

### WORKSHOPS

- Who is policy for?
- What is in policy?
- How is policy produced?
- How do we put policy into practice?
- Personal and group action planning

# Initial reflections: introduction

This introductory section consists of two workshops which provide a practical classroom- and school-focussed foundation on which to build work in the rest of the pack. It is intended to enable individuals, groups and teams to carry out an initial 'pre-course' review of their practice and policy with relation to equality and justice issues, in order to identify needs for development and training, and to provide a reference point to which participants can return to assess whether policy and practice has changed as a result of the course.

The workshops are designed around checklist questionnaires and can be used flexibly to relate the training materials to be found later in the pack to the classroom practice of teachers and to the policies and ethos of a school or college. Questions asked in the workshops are, in the main, open-ended and should result in reflection, discussion and, eventually, to action. The workshops should be used in the order given below as each leads directly onto the next. It is recommended that this section is completed before embarking on workshops in the "Curriculum issues" section.

It will be noted that the workshops deal with general educational practice and policy issues which will be relevant to all teachers and there may seem little which has a specific science focus. In "Looking at my classroom", the teacher is directed to review her/his practice against a range of general good-practice criteria which have implications for equality. Likewise in "Looking at our school/college", the team is asked to focus on institutional processes and policy issues in a wider community and societal context. This approach is consistent with the whole approach of the manual which stresses that science (and science education) needs to be seen in the wider contexts of community, society and world. However for those preferring to begin with a more 'science issues' focus, it might be more appropriate to work through the "Starters" section before attempting these workshops.

## THE WORKSHOPS

**1  Looking at my classroom – self review**: aims to enable individuals and groups to reflect on, and review, their existing classroom practice and approaches within the framework of 'race, equality and science teaching', through individual and group checklist activities.

**2  Looking at our school/college – team review**: aims to enable groups of teachers to reflect on, and review, existing policy and practice at team (or department) and institution level within the framework of 'race, equality and science teaching'.

# Looking at my classroom: self review

## PURPOSE
To enable individuals and groups to reflect on and review their existing classroom practice and approaches within the framework of 'race, equality and science teaching'.

## RESOURCES
Checklist and task sheets, pages 15-18. Paper, pens flipchart.

**Time: 90 minutes**

## PROCEDURE
Facilitator should introduce the session by stating the purpose and expected duration, and by providing some ideas of activities involved.

### Stage 1
Individuals given checklist sheets.

**1** Participants fill in/take notes on their responses to the questionnaires. **30 minutes**

### Stage 2
Small groups/teams given task sheet (page 18).

**2** Groups share their responses and discuss common approaches which have emerged from the initial questionnaires. Notes made for reporting back on question "How do we ensure we are adopting a common approach to…?" Each group is allocated or chooses an issue to report back response. **30 minutes**

**3** Reporter from each group reports to whole group on their discussions on the specified area of response. Facilitator takes flipchart notes on main points and leads discussion, invites comments and further discussion. **30 minutes**

**4** Participants keep initial responses as reference point for whole course.

### EVALUATION
It is important that evaluation takes place after each workshop. This exercise is, in itself, evaluative. However, there will be a need to assess the effectiveness of the "Initial reflections" process and materials. Evaluation can work on an individual basis or in small groups. Guidance notes, suggested approaches and a sample evaluation sheet can be found in Appendix 3 of this manual.

## NOTES FOR FACILITATORS
*This workshop is designed for flexible use in a number of different contexts. It can be used in a school or college as a starter activity for a whole school, team or department review. It can be used as the first session in a course in "Race, equality and science teaching" or as a pre-course checklist exercise which participants bring to the first session. The individual checklist has four sections: "The Learning Environment"; "Classroom Organisation, Teaching and Learning", "Resources for Learning" and "Expectations and Achievement", each includes a number of questions. Participants may wish to deal with each section separately and to discuss their responses – this is particularly appropriate if classroom observation is used (see below). Note that the questions are designed to be relevant for teachers in all phases – the aim of the exercise is to raise issues of quality of experience for all pupils or students. In a 'course' environment, cross-phase comparisons can form the basis for discussion in groups in Stage 2 of the workshop.*

*Participants should be asked to consider their responses to the questions in the light of the need for equality for all groups of pupils and for the teaching and learning of science in a multicultural society. It is important that the individual or team knows their class/school well; a useful preliminary to this exercise is to survey the pupil population with regard to ethnic background, gender balance, languages spoken, achievement and attainment levels by ethnic group/gender, level of provision of language and other support, and other relevant school-based data. Discussion of such data will raise issues to be addressed – all educational establishments are required by law to carry out ethnic monitoring, many others also systematically monitor student performance, racial incidents, etc.*

*If the workshop is being done as an in-school or a pre-course exercise, the checklist in Stage 1 can form the basis of active reflection following particular sessions, or can involve other colleagues through classroom observations. In schools where teacher appraisal includes self-review and regular classroom observation, this workshop will fit well into the ongoing process. Useful techniques include establishing pairs of 'critical friends' – two colleagues acting both as observers and observed, with 'results' discussed together, and 'triangulation'; here the observer's views are recorded alongside teacher and pupil/student perceptions. Subsequent discussion can take place on areas of consensus and differences of view. In Stage 2 the discussions will take place in a team situation where issues will be more directly related to immediate, practical needs. If used in a secondary school science department, Stage 2 may be crucial in enabling a team to review and coordinate its approaches before moving onto wider whole-school issues in the following workshop.*

*If the workshop is part of the first session of a course, the approach will necessarily be different, and possibly less active, in the initial stages. In Stage 1 the participants will be reflecting on their practice away from the classroom. This may result in a less immediate, but more dispassionate and objective, review. Similarly, in Stage 2, participants may be sharing reflections with colleagues from other institutions and phases of education. Here the facilitator should encourage groups to focus on common views and approaches which might be useful to all colleagues. In this situation, the exercise is more geared to identifying the training needs of the group, than the practical needs of a particular school. Discussions are further developed in the next workshop in this section, "Looking at our school/college".*

*In Stage 2, when groups are discussing the question on the task sheet, facilitators may wish to allocate one of the areas listed on the card for each group to report back on.*

# Looking at our school/college: team review

## PURPOSE

To enable groups of teachers to reflect on, and review, existing policy and practice at team (or department) and institution level within the framework of 'race, equality and science teaching'.

## RESOURCES

Checklist sheets, pages 19-21. Paper, pens, flipchart.

**Time: 80 minutes**

## PROCEDURE

Facilitator should introduce the session by stating the purpose and expected duration, and by providing some ideas of activities involved.

## ACTIVITIES

Groups of three or four are given checklist sheet.

**1** Groups of three or four are asked to discuss checklist provided. Participants share individual responses, views and experiences and notes are taken by a scribe on common experiences, consensus viewpoints and areas of dissent for reporting back to whole group.

**50 minutes**

**2** Each group reports back on responses and facilitator leads a whole-group discussion based on the common experiences and needs identified. **30 minutes**

## NOTES FOR FACILITATORS

*Like the previous workshop, this can equally well be carried out as an INSET workshop, or as a school-based development involving whole staff or teams. The procedure is simple in that groups are asked to discuss and respond to a series of questions on the checklist similar in format to the individual checklist in the previous workshop. However this workshop deals predominantly with policy and communication, rather than classroom practice issues. The questions, as they appear, may seem to be geared towards 'in-school' use. However, if they are used in an INSET session the aim is i) for individuals within groups to share the different experiences they will have, and ii) to respond in general terms to the issues. As an alternative, individuals may be asked to fill in the questionnaire, basing their responses on their own experiences first, and then to report back to their group.*

*The checklist is in two parts, "Policy issues" and "Sharing ideas and strategies", and addresses the institutional processes which can support or hinder policy development in this area. As the previous workshop concentrated on general practice criteria, rather than specific scientific concerns, this workshop takes a whole-school and community-based approach to policy review.*

## EVALUATION

It is important that evaluation takes place after each workshop. This exercise is, in itself, evaluative. However, there will be a need to assess the effectiveness of the "Initial reflections" process and materials. Evaluation can work on an individual basis or in small groups. Guidance notes, suggested approaches and a sample evaluation sheet can be found in Appendix 3 of this manual.

·········································································

# A checklist activity

Consider the following questions and consider your responses in the light of the need for equality for all groups of pupils and of teaching and learning science in a multicultural society.

**THE LEARNING ENVIRONMENT**                    **NOTES**

- How pleasant a place is my classroom for my pupils/students and I to work in?

- Are there lots of exciting 'things' in it?

- What range of materials is used in the classroom for decoration and display, e.g. drapes, plants, etc?

- What is the balance between pupils'/students' work and other materials in displays? How is this chosen?

- How are displays used by pupils/students and myself in learning?  Are they interactive?

- How do the displays reflect and build on all pupils'/students' everyday experiences and interests?

- How do the displays represent social, linguistic and cultural diversity?

- Do displays contain positive images and role models for all pupils/students? Do they challenge stereotypes and racism?

- Is the language in displays appropriate and easily understood?

**CLASSROOM ORGANISATION, TEACHING**          **NOTES**
**AND LEARNING**

- How is the seating planned, and who sits where?

- Who participates in classroom activities? What contributions do they make?

## STAGE 1: ACTIVITY 1                                TASK

..........................................................................................

- Who do I give attention, encouragement, praise and reprimands to?

- Which pupils/students do I involve in the management of my classroom?

- How are activity and learning groups formed and roles in them assigned?

- Is a variety of activities used in teaching and learning in my class?

- Do pupils/students have opportunities to work collaboratively and share ideas and experiences?

- Do activities build on, and value, the social, cultural and linguistic experiences of all pupils/students?

- Do I, and my pupils/students, discuss and challenge racist and sexist viewpoints and inequalities?

- What degree of responsibility do I give pupils/students for their own learning? Do I share and discuss the purpose and processes with them?

**RESOURCES FOR LEARNING**               NOTES

- What range of resources are available to pupils/students? Are they relevant and accessible to all?

- How are resources used by pupils/students and myself in learning? Are they interactive?

- How do the resources reflect and build on all pupils'/students' everyday experiences and interests?

- How do the resources represent social, linguistic and cultural diversity?

## STAGE 1: ACTIVITY 1       TASK

..............................................................................................

- Do resources contain positive images and role models for all pupils/students?
  Do they challenge stereotypes and racism?

- Is the language in resources appropriate and easily understood?

**EXPECTATIONS AND ACHIEVEMENT**       **NOTES**

- What are my expectations of individuals and groups in my class and how do I convey these?

- What are their expectations of themselves and how do I know this?

- How do I plan to enable pupils/students to recognise their own strengths and to promote their self-esteem?

- How do I recognise and deal with racist or sexist incidents in my classroom?

- How do I ensure that assessment fully enables pupils/students to demonstrate what they know, understand and can do?

- How do I monitor the performance of individuals and groups of black, bilingual and other pupils/students?

- How do I ensure that the language used in my classroom enables every individual to have equal access to the curriculum?

## STAGE 2: ACTIVITY 2 TASK

........................................................................................

You have spent some time responding to the checklist questions. In your groups, briefly share individual observations and responses on questions you found most challenging or interesting.

Then discuss the following question:

**How do we ensure that we are adopting a common approach to:**

- **the learning environment;**
- **the resources we use;**
- **our teaching and learning approaches;**
- **our classroom organisation;**
- **our assessment procedures;**
- **monitoring the attainment of individuals and groups;**
- **rewards, sanctions and behaviour;**
- **dealing with racist/sexist incidents;**
- **language development issues,**

**in order to ensure equality for all and effective teaching of science in a multicultural society?**

Finally, discuss further, and make brief notes on, your responses to one of the areas listed above for reporting back to the whole group.

........................................................................................

**ACTIVITY I**                                                                      **TASK**

# A checklist activity

Your team in your school/college is about to address issues of 'race, equality and science teaching'. You are asked to respond to the checklist below, sharing experiences and noting common approaches. You will be asked to report back on a specific issue, section or question which has challenged or interested the group. Prepare brief notes on this for reporting back to the whole group.

**POLICY AND PRACTICE ISSUES**                      **NOTES**

- Does our school/college have a policy on multicultural or anti-racist education?

- Is our policy in line with LEA policy or any other current developments?

- Are our policy approaches to rewards, sanctions and behaviour, and dealing with racist/sexist incidents consistent and fair to all people in the school?

- Do we have a policy for equal opportunities in staff recruitment? What guidelines are there on shortlisting and selection procedures?

- Does the school have a language policy?

- Has this been specifically applied to learning in science?

- How are the specific language needs of developing bilingual learners recognised and addressed?

- What mechanisms are there for supporting developing bilingual learners in mainstream classrooms?

- Do we encourage collaborative teaching and learning to support developing bilingual learners?

## ACTIVITY I                                              TASK

......................................................................................................

- How does the school/college monitor pupil achievement, particularly of black, bilingual and other groups of pupils/students? What are the criteria?

- How do new members of teaching and ancillary staff, probationers, supply teachers, students, etc. find out about policy approaches in this area?


## SHARING IDEAS AND STRATEGIES           NOTES


### ...IN THE SCHOOL/COLLEGE

- Who else in the school/college is, or might be, considering issues of equality and anti-racism?

- What mechanisms exist to promote good practice across the school/college?

- Where can colleagues share ideas about equality issues with each other?

- With whom do we wish to share ideas about equality within the school/college?

- What means should we use to share our ideas and inform others of our activities?

- How can pupils/students be involved in these considerations?


### ...IN THE COMMUNITY

- How do we seek the help and involvement of all parents?

- How do we seek the specific help and involvement of parents from minority ethnic groups?

- Can we make use of any support systems which exist within minority ethnic communities?

- How can/will governors be involved in initiatives in this area?

## ACTIVITY 1           TASK

..............................................................................................

### ...BETWEEN SCHOOLS        NOTES

- How could our (science) curriculum benefit from enabling young people from different environments or cultures to communicate directly with each other?

- Could our policies and practices benefit from such links?

- How could such links be established?

- Has anyone in our school/college established or considered establishing links with other schools in different parts of the UK or in different countries?

# Starters: introduction

This introductory section of the manual consists of three workshops, exploring basic issues which will underpin work on the rest of the manual. It is intended to enable teachers to explore their own perceptions of science, of science education and of culture and ethnicity against an anti-racist rationale and to find out 'where they are at' with regard to issues of science, racism and equality in education.

The workshops are designed to define the boundaries of what can, and should, be acheived in terms of awareness of issues in changes in policy and practice, which are covered in more detail in other sections. They also enable teachers to explore the philosophies and viewpoints underpinning all the activities in this manual. These are explained in more detail in the discussion paper and "Terms used in this manual" section contained in Appendices 1 and 2 of this manual, and in the handbook which accompanies these INSET materials.

It is recommended that the workshops are worked sequentially in the order shown , with "What is science?" preceding the other two, and that all three are worked through before going on to a number of issues raised here.

## THE WORKSHOPS

**1  What is science?** aims to enable teachers to clarify their ideas about the nature of science before embarking on a discussion of culture, ethnicity and anti-racism and their relation to science education, through small group consideration of viewpoints on science, individual reflection and plenary discussions.

**2  What  is culture?** aims to enable teachers to begin to consider the dynamic and changing relationship between culture and ethnicity; to reflect on the way that culture impinges on many aspects of life in Britain and elsewhere and to appreciate how the multicultural nature of society is a central resource for teachers of science, through individual reflection and group discussion activities around the title theme.

**3  What is science education for?** aims to enable teachers to appreciate science education in its wider human and social context; to indicate day-to-day examples of how this can occur and to begin to explore ways of responding to these issues in the classroom. The workshop uses role play and discussion exercises around stimulus materials provided.

# What is science?

## PURPOSE

To enable teachers to clarify their ideas about the nature of science before embarking on a discussion of culture, ethnicity and anti-racism and their relation to science education.

## RESOURCES

"Tropical area" sheets, page 30; task and statements, pages 31-32.
Candles/candle holders, matches. Paper, pens, flipchart.

**Time: 80 minutes**

## PROCEDURE

Facilitator should introduce the session by stating the purpose and expected duration, and by providing some ideas of activities involved.

## NOTES FOR FACILITATORS

*This workshop is quite specific in its purpose and provides a number of staged activities in order to explore the nature of science.*

## ACTIVITIES

### Stage 1

Groups given candle, matches. Individuals given "Tropical area" sheet – page 30.

**1** Participants look at a burning candle and record individually as many observations as they can.

**5 minutes**

**2** Report back all observations to group of three or four. Note similarities and differences in observations, but avoid criticism and/or explanations. **10 minutes**

**3** Individuals complete task sheet "A tropical area farm". **5 minutes**

**4** Report back ideas in group and discuss differences and similarities in responses. **10 minutes**

*Stage 1: the aim here is to show that even adults will make a variety of observations, give different reasons for what they see, draw different conclusions or have different ideas about what might happen in certain situations. This suggests that what scientists observe and explain is influenced by, among other things, their views of science. It is suggested that science has a social and economic context from which it should not be removed.*
*For the candle activity all observations are to be reported; notes made might also include some inferences, hypotheses, etc. (some discussion to clarify such terms as inference and hypothesis might be useful). The diversity of observations should be made apparent. Criticisms and/or explanations should be avoided in group discussion at this stage.*

*The "Tropical area" task sheet presents a context and suggests that science is being set and bound by this social context. Opportunity to discuss this point is important so that participants can begin to explore the social, economic and political nature of science. In groupwork, mixed primary/secondary or science/non-science groupings may be useful to ensure a variety of opinions which are not all 'straight science'. If this is not possible, then the facilitator may need to ensure a variation of views through sensitive intervention.*

### Stage 2

### TASK

To develop a personal view of science to act as a reference point for the rest of this workshop and throughout the training.

**5** Whole group discussion introduced by facilitator's question: "What were our responses to the previous activities – can they help us to consider:
**a** What are our personal views of science?
**b** How does this influence our teaching of science?"

**10 minutes**

**6** Individual task. Each participant to note down their own view of science. **5 minutes**

*Stage 2 follows on from previous discussions and suggests that views of science vary and that these views may influence – directly or indirectly – how and what they teach. The individual statements are written down and can be kept as a running record of their thoughts as they progress through these workshops.*

**Stage 3**

Each group of three or four given set of cards "Ideas about science" and task from pages 31-32.

**TASK**

To explore a range of different views of science and the social, economic and political contexts in which science operates.

**7** Groups discuss cards. Decide collectively on the statement the group agrees with most and the one disagreed with most. Put the rest on a continuum. Individuals can make notes on own views on a separate copy of the sheet provided. Alternatively the task could be changed into sorting the cards into piles of *agree*, *disagree* or *not sure*. Individuals can also be given the statements on a sheet on which they can record their own views.                                          **25 minutes**

**8** Individuals consider and make notes on the question: "How does your view of science influence your approach to anti-racism and anti-sexism in teaching science?"                                          **10 minutes**

(At this stage facilitators may wish either to return to a whole group discussion to share persectives, or to end the workshop now.)

---

**EVALUATION**

It is important that evaluation takes place after each workshop. It can take place on an individual basis or in small groups. Guidance notes, suggested approaches and a sample evaluation sheet can be found in Appendix 3 of this manual.

---

*Stage 3: the nature of science is challenged in the card activity. The statements range between views of science as 'truth', to science as a way of 'viewing the world'. If science is seen as a way of 'viewing' then teachers will be more willing to accept the social, economic and political elements of science. This view is crucial in considering an anti-racist perpective in science education and these activities invite teachers to consider if their view of science allows for such a perspective. If science is a 'way of viewing', then observation and perceptions are influenced by factors such as background, class, gender, ethnicity and the values of our society or community. There may be, however, various ways in which teaching science can be consistent with an anti-racist perspective. If teachers believe that their view is not being accepted, then they may, rightly, refuse to consider arguments further.*

*Acknowledgement: activities and materials in this workshop adapted and taken, with permission, from* Issues in Science Education: Developing an Anti-racist Approach, An In-service Discussion Pack *by Pauline Hoyle, 1987.*

# What is science education about?

## PURPOSE
• to enable teachers to appreciate science education in its wider human and social context;
• to indicate day-to-day examples of how this can occur;
• to begin to explore ways of responding to these issues in the classroom.

## RESOURCES
Memo A: memo, page 33; Letter B: page 34.
O.H.P.; paper; pens, flipchart

**Time: 70–90 minutes**

## PROCEDURE
Facilitator should introduce the session by stating the purpose and expected duration, and by providing some ideas of activities involved.

## ACTIVITIES
### Stage 1
Scenario: a teacher gets a memo from her headteacher questioning her handling of a topic in science.

## TASK
To prepare the teacher's response or statement before her meeting with the headteacher.

1  In groups (of two, three or four) participants read and discuss memo A and underlying issues involved.
**15 minutes**

2  Groups prepare a response or list of points to be made by the teacher to her headteacher for the meeting.
**15 minutes**

3  Report back and pose question for discussion "What is science education about?" Record responses on flip-chart/O.H.P.
**10 minutes**

OR

3  Role play the meeting between headteacher and the teacher involved using two participants. Rest of the group observes and then whole group discuss responses to role play. Question posed for discussion "What is science education about?"
**30 minutes**

### Stage 2
Letter B is handed out to individuals.

4  Groups read and briefly discuss letter B and underlying issues involved.
**10 minutes**

## NOTES FOR FACILITATORS:
*The two letters provide two contexts in which science education can be considered. The first, which might be considered 'reductionist', asks whether science can or should be taught with reference to the wider human and social context. The second challenges teachers by presenting a real social context within which science and education might operate. Both are likely to provoke strong opinions and a lively debate is to be encouraged. However, facilitators should try to ensure that participants stick to the tasks specified so that there can be positive and practical outcomes. To facilitate a more flexible response, an alternative task has been provided to enable role play to occur.*

*In the alternative provided for 3) two of the participants can role play the meeting between the teacher and headteacher. These colleagues need to be primed before the workshop and given some background information; they may wish to discuss the personalities of the two with the facilitator. A third role could be provided by extending the role play to include a meeting with the complaining parent. There are several ways to follow up the role play. The first is for the other participants simply to discuss the issues as suggested. Another response is to 'hot seat' or interview one or both of the players in their role about what was said, action taken and motives, etc. However, it is important that discussion starts and finishes with the question "What is science education about?"*

**5** Report back and pose the question in 3) again – has this changed/affected their responses? Discuss this with whole group referring to, and amending, notes. During discussion, pose the additional question "What can be done to further explore the contexts of science in day-to-day teaching?"– record responses. General discussion and responses to the contexts provided. **20 minutes**

---

**EVALUATION**

It is important that evaluation takes place after each workshop. It can take place on an individual basis or in small groups. Guidance notes, suggested approaches and a sample evaluation sheet can be found in Appendix 3 of this manual.

---

*The grouping of participants is also important. Primary colleagues and those who are used to working in a cross-curricular way may consider the second letter more relevant to their approach to the curriculum with its challenge to educate the whole child 'to be human'. Secondary and more specialist science teachers may find the challenge of the first scenario more stimulating in its stark portrayal of different priorities within a secondary school. It is important, therefore, that the facilitator considers whether a cross-phase/cross-curricular approach to grouping is more applicable to get a range of viewpoints, or whether a specialist department or faculty requires a different approach.*

# Culture in the classroom

## PURPOSE
• to begin to consider the dynamic and changing relationship between culture and ethnicity;
• to reflect on the way that culture impinges on many aspects of life in Britain and elsewhere;
• to appreciate how the multicultural nature of society is a central resource for teachers of science.

## RESOURCES
Task sheet page 35, O.H.P., page 36. Paper, pens, flipchart, O.H.P.

**Time: 50 minutes**

## PROCEDURE
Facilitator should introduce the session by stating the purpose and expected duration, and by providing some ideas of activities involved.

## NOTES FOR FACILITATORS
*For many teachers, approaches in education to equality and justice are likely to be encompassed in the term 'multicultural education'. Yet many participants are likely to find thinking about, and defining culture and related concepts challenging. Sensitivity is required to ensure honest and comfortable responses. Participants should come to see how difficult it is to define 'culture' and 'ethnicity'; how all people's needs and aspirations are interrelated and constantly changing and that a person's culture is a dynamic and changing quality related to their age, class, ethnicity, religion, family, gender, sexual orientation and ability. Understanding this is central to any attempt to be child centred in education and to addressing the hidden curriculum of this workshop – central to this publication – a challenge to racism and the assumptions it builds on. Facilitators themselves, should be familiar with the terms used; a starting point for this can be found in Appendix 2 in which terms used in this manual are discussed, but more in-depth reading may be required. The Appendix can also be used as a handout or as a discussion document to support this workshop.*

## ACTIVITIES
### Stage 1

### TASK
To brainstorm and discuss viewpoints and images of culture.

**1** In whole group, brainstorm manifestations and meanings of the word 'culture'; record these. Ask if there are any comments/surprising aspects on the list.
**10 minutes**

**2** Pairs choose and discuss two items from the brainstorm which may impinge on the teaching of science. **5 minutes**

(The word list to be referred to again at the end of the workshop.)

*Stage 1: in the initial brainstorm do not be concerned if things go quiet for a while! If this occurs, or if the brainstorm is focusing purely on multicultural aspects, then it might be useful to throw in a few lighthearted examples, for example, Yorkshire Pudding, bagpipes, pop music, etc.*

## Stage 2

Participants are each given a sheet with five statements about culture and ethnicity.

### TASK

To reach common understanding and definitions of the term 'ethnicity'.

**3** Individuals to think about whether they agree or disagree with these statements. Stress that there are no right answers. Individuals then write down what they think is meant by the term 'ethnicity'. **5 minutes**

**4** Pairs share their ideas and discuss their definitions, trying to reach a collective definition if possible. **5 minutes**

**5** In whole group, pairs share their definitions and discuss responses. **10 minutes**

## Stage 3

### TASK

To relate issues of culture and ethnicity to teachers' own classroom practice.

### ACTIVITIES

**6** Facilitator poses the question on O.H.P. original:
"Can you think of examples when culture or ethnicity have contributed to your teaching of science?
Try to identify:
- a topic;
- a specific classroom activity;
- a practical investigation".
Give an example to start if required.
Discussion takes place in pairs – refer participants to list of brainstormed words and concepts around culture in Stage 1.

**7** Pairs share examples with the whole group.

*Stage 2: the activity sheet is designed to stimulate deeper thinking about concepts of culture and ethnicity. The questions are deliberately designed to challenge ideas of culture in a subtle, non-threatening way. However, if the exercise proves difficult, then the background glossary sheet contained in Appendix 2 of this manual might be useful as a further stimulus for discussion. Participants may be asked to discuss their own responses to the viewpoints and definitions of culture and ethnicity contained in the Appendix.*

*Stage 3: examples provided in introducing this task should ideally come directly from own experience. Simple starting examples provided could include using fruits from around the world to look at seed size and number, etc.*

*OR*

*Starting a topic on light with reference to religious celebrations such as Diwali, Hannuka etc. Note, however, that these are superficial examples to stimulate discussion and not suggested approaches. More valuable would be examples which build directly on pupils' own cultural experiences.*

### EVALUATION

It is important that evaluation takes place after each workshop. It can take place on an individual basis or in small groups. Guidance notes, suggested approaches and a sample evaluation sheet can be found in Appendix 3 of this manual.

## A TROPICAL AREA FARM

The farm in question is in a tropical area where plant growth is prolific. Traditionally the wild plants are used by local people for seasonal grazing, food supply and as medicinal herbs.

The farmer has worked hard to create fields to grow grain, but the surrounding areas of wild plants tend to grow rapidly and take over parts of the grain fields.

The farmer consults an agricultural adviser, and sprays the area around the grain fields with a chemical which reduces wild plant growth. The following year there is a bumper grain crop.

What do you think the situation will be like in a few years' time?

What do you think of this use of science?

# Ideas about science

You have been provided with a set of statements which give different ideas about science.

The task is for the group to decide together which statement you agree with most and which you most disagree with. The rest of the statements should then be placed along a continuum between these two.

OR

The group to sort, together, all the statements into three piles – *agree*, *disagree* and *not sure*.

The statements are also contained on a sheet on which you can record your own views regardless of whether or not they are the same as those of your group.

## STATEMENTS

> Through science, we will eventually learn the real truth about how the natural world works.

> Scientific knowledge is different from other forms of knowledge because it is based on observations rather than on speculation.

> Every culture has its own kind of science. Just because some other culture's science is different from ours, does not mean that the science of that culture is less valid.

> Scientific statements can only be known to be true if they can be checked by observations.

> Scientific observations are never totally objective.

Since scientific theories are creations of the human mind they do not necessarily describe things the way they really are.

Our scientific ideas will probably appear as different to people living in the year 3000 as the scientific ideas of the Middle Ages appear to us.

Scientific theories and concepts affect what scientists observe.

Science is one of the ways which people have developed to understand and make sense of the world.

What counts as scientific evidence and explanations depends on the cultural values of the people involved in the science.

Scientific theories are products of the human imagination.

The observations and theories are influenced by their culture and its values.

Science is one of the purest forms of knowledge because it is objective, value-free and rational.

Science is the form of knowledge which exists outside of, and free from, the influences of culture.

## St Somewhere's School
### Roundhere Road
### Localton
### Nearshire
*Headmaster: Mr Barry Jones BSc. PGCE. MA*

**MEMO**

From: Headmaster

**To:** Jane Renton

Jane,

This morning I had a parent on the phone complaining about your science lesson yesterday. From what I understand it was a lesson on food and nutrition. The parent suggested that you spent an inordinate amount of time talking and discussing with pupils the problems of poverty and hunger in Africa. The parent thought it must have been distressing for the youngsters, but the main point he wanted to make was that it was unnecessary and irrelevant to the science work you were doing at the time. I have to say I tend to agree with him. You will appreciate that with the current pressures on all of us to implement the National Curriculum, anything which is not directly relevant to the learning of science must be avoided.

I also noticed, looking through the scheme of work on food which Derek was able to provide me, that this sort of digression is neither necessary or expected.

Perhaps we can have a brief chat tomorrow so that I can ring the parent back and reassure him.


*Barry Jones*


Barry Jones

*Dear Teacher,*

*I am a survivor of a concentration camp. My eyes saw what no man should witness:*

*gas chambers built by learned engineers; children poisoned by educated physicians; infants killed by trained nurses; women and babies shot by high-school and college graduates.*

*So I am suspicious of education.*

*My request is:*

*help your students to become human. Your efforts must never produce learned monsters, skilled psychopaths, educated Eichmanns.*

*Reading, writing and arithmetic are important only if they serve to make our children more human.*

## STAGE 2: ACTIVITY 3 TASK

........................................................................................

Read the following statements.
In each case decide whether you agree or disagree with them.

| | Agree | Disagree |
|---|---|---|
| **1** Britain is a multicultural society. | _____ | _____ |
| **2** Britain is a multiethnic society. | _____ | _____ |
| **3** People of different age groups in a multiethnic society belong to different cultures. | _____ | _____ |
| **4** People in a multiethnic society can share the same culture. | _____ | _____ |
| **5** Ethnicity is about people's beliefs, religions, origins and appearance. | _____ | _____ |

What do you understand by the term ethnicity?

## ETHNICITY IS

# CULTURE AND ETHNICITY

In pairs, think of examples when culture or ethnicity have contributed to your teaching of science.

Try to identify:

- a topic;
- a specific classroom activity;
- a practical investigation.

Discuss these and select one particularly interesting example to share with the whole group.

# Curriculum issues: introduction

This section is central in terms of addressing a range of practical and theoretical issues concerned with science, equality and anti-racism in education. It is intended to:

• enable teachers to explore, in some depth, issues of curriculum content, contexts and processes in science education for equality and justice;
• provide opportunities to challenge preconceptions and attitudes and share relevant perspectives and practice.

The section reflects the view of the authors that the curriculum should be at the centre of any strategies to combat racism and provide equality of access and opportunity in education. In the context of this manual, that means the science curriculum. The section has been divided into what we have called (with no apologies to the National Curriculum) 'core' and 'foundation' workshops. The first three 'core' workshops are those we recommend are used first. These build, in various ways, on the issues explored in the "Starters" and "Initial Reflections" sections and will lead participants to ask questions which can be addressed in other workshops in this section. We suggest that the three – "Science for people", "Principles into practice" and "Race and racism" – are worked through in the order they are listed below. The central workshop for the whole section is the "Race and racism" workshop. Whilst the first two workshops continue to build on the experiences and viewpoints of participants, enabling them to explore ideas in a relatively unstructured way, the "Race and Racism" workshop is clearly structured in a way which requires clear analysis. The workshop requires teachers to consider the nature of race and racism and their views of these, together with the implications and effects of teacher expectations and assumptions of pupils based on stereotyped notions of culture, race and class.

Work on the core can then lead to a number of routes through the other 'foundation' workshops in the section. The 'foundation' workshops themselves can be roughly divided into 'process' and 'context' categories. The 'process' workshops are concerned with the approaches to the curriculum and lead on most naturally from the "Me and my pupils" section. These are "Language and learning", "Groupings in the classroom", Teaching and learning for equality" and "Assessment". The 'context' workshops are more concerned with the frameworks and content of the curriculum and approaches to it. These are the "Images in science", "Science systems", "Science themes" and "National Curriculum"

workshops. Facilitators should not feel constrained when planning a route through this section. However, we would suggest that the "National Curriculum" workshop would be most effective at the end of this section so that participants can build on the awareness gained of issues and opportunities in the planning process provided.

## THE WORKSHOPS

**CORE** (in recommended sequential order)

**Science for people** aims to enable participants to reflect on personal experiences of science and to relate these reflections to planning topics, which value and build on the scientific experiences of pupils and of people worldwide. This is done through personal and group reflection and discussion activities.

**Principles into practice** aims to help teachers to address and discuss a range of viewpoints on how the science curriculum can be developed to enable equality issues to be addressed and implemented in the classroom through discussing viewpoints and using classroom scenarios provided.

**Race and racism** aims to enable teachers to begin to explore how issues of race and racism might affect the teaching and learning of science in classroom with a view to:

• considering 'race' as a discredited scientific concept;
• recognising the need to challenge racist behaviour and practices, attitudes and assumptions.

The workshop uses a structured, interactive tape activity and group discussion.

**FOUNDATION** ('route' to be planned by facilitator – see route planner diagram)

## 'PROCESS' WORKSHOPS

**Teaching and learning for equality** aims to explore ways in which teaching and learning strategies in science can help promote equality, by group discussion and exploration of active learning strategies.

**Language and learning** aims to consider ways in which language promotes learning in science, and why language and learning is an important aspect of developing equality in classrooms, through group discussion and analysis of classroom activities.

**Assessment** aims to share and raise awareness of strategies of promoting justice and equality in assessment and to highlight principles of equality in the issues of assessment. This workshop uses practical case studies and pupil profiles to establish principles through group activities.

**Groupings in the classroom** aims to explore the implications for equality of opportunity and access to the curriculum, of how pupils/students are grouped in the classroom, through context card activities based on realistic classroom scenarios.

## 'CONTEXT' WORKSHOPS

**Images in science** through the use of photograph activities, aims to enable teachers to challenge preconceptions regarding science/scientists and people in other countries; to show positive images of people around the world involved in scientific activities involving sophisticated knowledge and processes, and to explore how photographs might be used in classrooms to explore issues in science.

**Science themes** through a simple group planning exercise, aims to encourage cross-curricular thinking around science-based units of work, and to explore the assertions that:

• introducing global dimensions and issues can make the science content more relevant for students;
• science taught within a more holistic framework can increase student interest in the science itself.

**Science systems** aims to look at two agricultural systems and explore the impact of these on people and the environment; to look at the science in each system and to begin to think about, and explore, the underlying values, and to explore the view that 'reductionist' (Western) science often results in environmental degradation and increased poverty when applied in developing countries. Group and plenary activities are used.

**National Curriculum** aims to build confidence that opportunities exist to promote principles of equality and justice through the National Curriculum by:

• showing that links exist between National Curriculum programmes of study, relevant attainment targets and the cross-curricular multicultural dimensions of the National Curriculum;
• exploring strategies for translating such links into schemes of work. The workshop uses a curriculum mapping tool for small group and plenary activities.

# Science for people

## PURPOSE

To enable participants:
- to reflect on personal experiences of science;
- to reflect on the methods used by teachers in discovering the scientific experiences pupils bring into the classroom;
- to explore how these experiences can be used to:
  - positively develop a child's self esteem;
  - progress all pupils' understanding of science;
  - portray science as an everyday worldwide activity.

## RESOURCES

Task/checklist sheet, page 59; case studies, pages 60-62; handout, pages 63-64. Paper, pens, flipchart.

**Time: 105 mins**

## PROCEDURE

Facilitator should introduce the session by stating the purpose and expected duration, and by providing some ideas of activities involved.

## NOTES FOR FACILITATORS

*This workshop provides a useful follow up to the "Starter section" workshops, "What is science?" and "What is science education for?" and asks participants to explore these questions in relation to their own experiences. These are drawn from experiences as far back into their childhood memory as possible. It then extends these considerations into looking at the implications for the curriculum and asks teachers to respond positively to their own pupils' experiences and those of people worldwide. The idea that science is an everyday activity of which everybody of all ages, cultures and backgrounds has valid experiences, should emerge. This idea should inform teachers' approaches to the teaching and learning of science in their classrooms. Exploring science in these personal, human and cultural contexts can go a long way towards developing an anti-racist approach which positively acknowledges and builds on students' cultural experiences and global perspectives – as well as encouraging teachers to begin challenging specialist and reductionist views of science.*

## ACTIVITIES
### Stage I

Exploring teachers' experiences.

1–3 facilitator poses question a), b) and c) in turn. In pairs, participants discuss and note down responses. Feedback to whole group takes place at each stage, facilitator draws out main points (see notes).

**15 minutes each activity**

I    question **a** "Think back to when you first realised you were doing science – make a list of experiences."

*Stage 1: explores the personal experiences of teachers and links these with views of science. Each question posed is followed by pair or small group discussion, note-taking and reporting back. In a whole group discussion session, facilitators should try to draw out common factors and raise possible issues, as in the notes which follow.*

*Activity 1, question a "Think back to when you first realised you were doing science – make a list of experiences."*
*Possible answers: "In Junior School we had a nature table"; "A candle was burned in a jam jar"; "Growing crystals", etc.*

*Guidance: participants can be asked to think about early secondary experiences, or those at junior and infant school, if they can remember that far back. If any comments that pertain to everyday activities emerge (e.g. "We baked bread"), these can be used to clarify activity 2, question b.*

**2** question **b** "Informed by your present knowledge and experience, can you list some science experiences you have had from this moment in time back to early childhood?"

*Activity 2, question b "Informed by your present knowledge and experience, can you list some science experiences you have had from this moment in time back to early childhood?"*

*Possible answers: home experience: baking bread, changing a motor-car wheel, building a Lego model, sand/water play, exploring a wood, etc.*

*Guidance: cultural, gender and class influences may emerge from the lists produced in this activity. These could be noted for reference during final plenary. Be prepared for some challenge to the answers given, eg. "They're not science". Turn this into a discussion point – perhaps looking at a science process model which refers to science investigation processes such as observing, hypothesising, planning, communicating, carrying out, interpreting and evaluating; can these refer to the activities listed?*

**3** question **c** "What did school science ever do for you?"

*Activity 3, question c "What did school science ever do for you?"*

*Possible answers: "Allowed me to go to university", "Got me a job in teaching", "Turned me off science", "Gave me a hobby", etc.*

*Guidance : like the* **Monty Python** *question "What did the Romans ever do for us?", this is designed to provoke both positive and negative responses which will relate to personal experiences. Gender issues, particularly regarding the physical sciences and technology, may emerge and should be discussed sensitively with regard to the power relationships involved and the attitudes/expectations of teachers. Can lead to a discussion on teacher expectations of students now – girls, black students, etc.*

**4** Facilitator poses question **d** "Why teach science?" Participants discuss and note down responses. Feedback to whole group and facilitator takes notes. Facilitator provides handout on "Why teach science?" and leads discussion, noting similarities/differences between participants' responses and views on handout.

**15 minutes**

*Activity 4, question d "Why teach science?"*

*Guidance: to this question participants should be constructing their own definition of the purposes of teaching science based on the discussions above. In the ensuing discussion the facilitator may like to use the handout sheet which provides some possible views for comparison. Discussion can address whether the statements produced relate to the experiences of students and of people portrayed in the kinds of science contexts and images used in classrooms – who is shown doing science? What kind of science are they doing? and so on.*

## Stage 2
Exploring pupils' experiences.

**5** Facilitator gives out copies of case studies. Groups of three or four discuss these using questions on task sheet as focus for discussion. **30 minutes**

**6** Each group chooses one card to report back on in plenary session. Facilitator notes down common strategies for drawing and building on pupils' experiences. **15 minutes**

### EVALUATION
It is important that evaluation takes place after each workshop. It can take place on an individual basis or in small groups. Guidance notes, suggested approaches and a sample evaluation sheet can be found in Appendix 3 of this manual.

*In Stage 2, case studies, in the form of profiles of pupils, are used to consider the implications of pupils' experiences for the way the science curriculum is constructed. Each group can be given a set of case studies, or be given a specific one to report back on. Alternatively all groups could be given the same case study and responses compared. Discussion takes place around the questions provided, and the following guidelines might be useful for plenary discussion.*

*For effective learning to take place a pupil's existing concepts and models of understanding must be explored, challenged and extended. Facilitators should encourage participants to consider how this can be done effectively. For a black pupil, the received perceptions of science may place her own ethnic or cultural group well down in the pecking order of success. The pupil may also not be accustomed to having her experiences valued by the class. The teacher, possibly with a different set of cultural and life experiences, should consider how she can draw upon all pupils' relevant experiences and use them in a way that develops pupils' self esteem, as well as progressing their understanding of science. Finally teachers should be encouraged to consider how pupils from a range of cultural and ethnic backgrounds can be used to help portray science as an everyday, worldwide activity.*

*For the final question on the task sheet provided – drawing up a checklist – facilitators may alternatively like to provide participants with the supporting sheet "possible inclusions in checklist for drawing on pupils' experiences".*

# Principles into practice

## PURPOSE
To enable teachers to address and discuss a range of viewpoints on how the science curriculum can be developed to enable equality issues to be addressed and implemented in the classroom.

## RESOURCES
Task and statements, pages 65–66; task and scenarios, pages 67–71. Paper, pens, flipchart, O.H.P.

**Time: 105 minutes**

## PROCEDURE
Facilitator should introduce the session by stating the purpose and expected duration, and by providing some ideas of activities involved.

## ACTIVITIES
### Stage 1
Participants (in groups of three or four) given set of statements which have been made by teachers and which refer to possible principles for 'education for equality'.

## TASK
To consider and prioritise principles for equality based on statements.

1 In groups (of two, three or four) participants to collectively sort statements into ones the group agree or disagree with or are not sure about. Blank cards are available for groups to add their own principles.

**20 minutes**

2 Groups consider top three statements only. For each, decide how the principle described could be recognised in practice in the classroom or school. Note responses.

**25 minutes**

3 Groups report back to the whole group with response to top statement. (Facilitator can also collect notes in, collate them and re-circulate later so each person has a full set of the criteria developed.)

**10 minutes**

## NOTES FOR FACILITATOR
*Responses to the exercise will depend on the nature of the institutions in which teachers work. Facilitators should consider this when forming groups. As a general guideline, if general principles are being addressed, then cross-phase groups might be appropriate; if more specific criteria are required then single-phase or key-stage groups might be more appropriate.*

*More specific points or questions emerging might include:*
- *"Do teachers really make such statements?"*
- *"What else do they say?"*
- *"How relevant/realistic are the scenarios and statements?"*

*It is important that the validity of these is established to ensure that the workshop is able to address its purpose:*
- *"Why do the pupils and teachers in the scenarios react as they do?"*

*This question enables issues of racism, etc. to come out overtly during the discussion:*
- *"Where is the 'science?'", "Aren't these scenarios* humanities *examples?"*

*Previous workshops in the "Starters" section should have begun to address this question:*
- *"How do the participants themselves plan relevant human contexts in their teaching of science?"*

*This will differ greatly depending on phase, the nature of the school/department, etc.; handled sensitively this can enable good practice examples to emerge from the participants themselves:*
- *"What is anti-racist about such approaches?"*

*Equating anti-racism with aspects of already existing 'good practice' further opens up questions of context, access and achievement, leading on to other workshops in this section.*

## Stage 2

Participants given set of scenarios (suggest five selected from those available) per group of three or four, which describe classroom practice situations.

## TASK

To apply principles and criteria developed in stage 1 to classroom practice.

**4** Groups discuss scenarios and decide which principles and criteria from Stage 1 apply to each.     **30 minutes**

**5** Each group selects one scenario and prepares brief notes for reporting back to the whole group.

OR

Groups note ideas about how teacher(s) and pupils in one scenario selected could further develop the theme to ensure that more principles/criteria are addressed, or that they are addressed in more depth.     **10 minutes**

**6** Groups report back. Facilitator can draw out main points onto an O.H.P. or flipchart, or could collect in notes made and re-circulate. Discussion should enable participants to relate their own practice and to give examples similar to those described in the scenarios.

**10 minutes**

---

### EVALUATION

It is important that evaluation takes place after each workshop. It can take place on an individual basis or in small groups. Guidance notes, suggested approaches and a sample evaluation sheet can be found in Appendix 3 of this manual.

---

# Race and racism

## PURPOSE

To begin to explore how issues of race and racism might affect the teaching and learning of science in the classroom with a view to:

- considering 'race' as a discredited scientific concept;
- recognising the need to challenge racist behaviour and practices, attitudes and assumptions.

## RESOURCES

Task sheet, page 72; transcript pages 73–74; reference sheet, pages 75–76; handout, page 77; O.H.P. 1and 2, pages 78–79. Paper, pens flipchart, tape recorder and blank tape, O.H.P.

**Time: 80 minutes**

## PROCEDURE

Facilitator should introduce the session by stating the purpose and expected duration, and by providing some ideas of activities involved.

## ACTIVITIES

Scenario: a conversation between a teacher and a deputy headteacher has been recorded as part of a collaborative review or appraisal session.

## TASK

To analyse the conversation in discussion, drawing out issues relating to racism and equality.

1 Play tape to whole group (or participants read/role play transcript of conversation). While this is happening participants make brief notes on what issues they think are being raised by the speakers. **10 minutes**

2 In whole group, brainstorm and produce a list of issues emerging. Facilitator to note these on flipchart or O.H.P. **10 minutes**

3 Each group of three or four takes ownership of one issue listed – each group should take a different issue. They should then discuss the issues around the questions on the workshop card namely:
- Why is it important to take action?
- What would you do about it?
- Have you experienced anything similar?
- What did you do?
- How did it work out? **20 minutes**

4 In plenary, small group reporters provide feedback on discussions and colleagues are invited to comment on or discuss the responses (at this stage it may be useful to play the tape again). Facilitator to pose the question:

"Can you think of any issues from the tape that have not been identified or mentioned initially?" Add these to the list. Final key question for discussion: "Where do

## NOTES FOR FACILITATORS

*For this workshop, preparation is very important. The workshop materials include a transcript of a conversation between two teachers following a lesson taught by one and observed by the other as part of a review or appraisal process. It is recommended that, prior to the workshop, a tape is made of two colleagues, in role, reading this script, to be played at the beginning of the workshop. If this is not possible then two participants in the workshop could role play and read the script. If a small group or team of teachers is using the materials then it might be more appropriate for them to read the transcript together and to do the task in 3) with several issues raised – possibly the ones highlighted for facilitators in the script and reference sheet.*

*The issues raised during the transcript are sensitive and it may require facilitators to raise relevant points and respond to questions, although it is preferable if the issues emerge from the participants themselves. Hence the "Reference sheet" has been produced to aid this. This is cross-referenced to particular quotes in the transcript; these are highlighted in the script in bold type. Reference is also made to other relevant workshops in this manual which may be of use in following up a particular issue and to sections in the discussion document contained as an appendix to the manual.*

*"Race and racism" is likely to be the most sensitive, but also the most important workshop in setting the overall framework of combatting racism and providing equality of opportunity and access in education. Some of the manifestations of racism highlighted in the transcript are relatively subtle, in comparison with more obvious racist incidents such as violent physical or verbal abuse. It is important that racism at all levels is dealt with and discussed.*

*The Working Party's stance on these issues is unequivocal and is contained in the discussion paper (Appendix 1) and addressed in more detail in the handbook which accompanies this manual. In short, however, it can be summed up as:*

these viewpoints and practices in the script come from?'' Note down responses on O.H.P./flipchart.

**30 minutes**

**5** Bearing in mind previous discussions, small groups are asked to come up with a definition of racism. These to be reported back and displayed. Facilitator sums up by showing O.H.P. with statement on race, going through, and giving out, handout sheets on race issues (and transcript of tape for reference, if required).

**30 minutes**

---

**EVALUATION**

This workshop is central to the ''Curriculum issues'' section and can lead on to work in other workshops. The evaluation should be to enable participants to identify and prioritise their own needs regarding the ''next step'' in the training process. Individual responses can be made but small group discussion fed back to a plenary would also be useful. Facilitators to take notes and plan the next stages based on this discussion.

---

• *Racism in many forms is pervasive in society and educational establishments and has a detrimental effect on pupils' learning, achievement and social development;*

• *'Race' as a scientific concept applied to humans has no biological or genetic validity. It is on such false definitions that racist beliefs and practices have often been built and supported;*

• *Teachers of science have a duty to work towards the elimination of racism in all its forms – in classrooms, institutions and the community.*

*Although alternative views will, naturally, emerge from a discussion exercise such as this, it is important to stress that this, and other workshops, are built around the above assumptions and teachers should be made aware of this.*

# Teaching and learning for equality

## PURPOSE

To explore ways in which teaching and learning strategies in science can help promote equality.

## RESOURCES

O.H.P. , page 80; task and cartoons, pages 81-83; task and list, page 84. Pens, paper, flipchart, O.H.P.

**Time: 100 minutes**

## PROCEDURE

Facilitator should introduce the session by stating the purpose and expected duration, and by providing some ideas of activities involved.

## ACTIVITIES

**1** Participants asked briefly to write down their own ideas about ways in which teaching and learning strategies/styles could promote equality. These are then kept for later. **10 minutes**

**2** Facilitator talks through the O.H.P. original on "Teaching and learning strategies to promote equality". **5 minutes**

**3** Small groups of three or four given set of cartoons of teaching and learning situations to analyse. Group chooses one or two of the scenarios shown (or adds their own) and is responsible for reporting back on these. Discussion is around questions on task sheet. **20 minutes**

**4** Feedback from small groups to plenary. Other participants add any extra comments. Facilitator can make notes of main points emerging. **20 minutes**

**5** Participants given sheet with list of "Teaching and learning strategies". Groups are asked to identify which have the potential for promoting equality and why. **15 minutes**

**6** Groups are asked to design a poster showing how a classroom might be organised to promote teaching and learning for equality. **15 minutes**

**7** Groups present their poster to the rest of the group to discuss. Facilitator asks participants to compare comments with their original ideas. **15 minutes**

## NOTES FOR FACILITATORS

*This workshop is intended to demonstrate that good practice in teaching science, using a variety of active and independent teaching and learning strategies, can help provide access to the curriculum and promote equality in the classroom. This builds on the viewpoint that anti-racist education is not only about the content of the curriculum, but also about the educational processes involved. It also suggests that the processes of science education, in particular, can promote equality – a view which is expanded in sections of the handbook.*

*Activities 1 & 2 involve the establishment of the importance of teaching and learning strategies in promoting equality. For activity 2, it is recommended that the facilitator is familiar with the principles outlined on the O.H.P. original prior to the workshop.*

*Activities 3–7 involve the development of more specific strategies for classroom practice based around cartoon scenarios and a poster task. For activity 3, the cartoons provided can be used or photo examples taken from other materials (such as T.E.S.). Be careful when selecting such images, however, that they address positive images of gender, ethnicity, etc. (Similar cartoons are available in the* Children's Learning in Science *project materials, but these do not address issues of positive images.)*

*In Acivity 5, groups are asked to relate the equality principles explored and developed with a list of teaching and learning strategies. This can be provided in the form of a handout or O.H.P. displayed, and notes made on the sheet.*

### EVALUATION

It is important that evaluation takes place after each workshop. It can take place on an individual basis or in small groups. Guidance notes, suggested approaches and a sample evaluation sheet can be found in Appendix 3 of this manual.

# Language and learning in science workshop

## PURPOSE
• to consider ways in which language promotes learning in science;
• to consider why language and learning is an important aspect of developing equality in classrooms.

## RESOURCES
O.H.P. 1, page 85; task and statements, pages 86–87; task sheet, page 88; task 4A sheets (childrens' writing), pages 89–93; 4B sheets (breathing), pages 94–96; 4C sheets (hotness), page 97; O.H.P. 2, page 98; handouts, pages 99-100.  Paper, pens, flipchart, newspaper, sticky tape, O.H.P.

**Time : 90 minutes**

## PROCEDURE
Facilitator should introduce the session by stating the purpose and expected duration, and by providing some ideas of activities involved.

## NOTES FOR FACILITATORS
*This workshop is very practical and the facilitator should ensure that all the background material is available. Some of the material is simply for use as stimulus, other sheets can be used as handouts to support the workshop. Participants should be encouraged to use their initial responses to the question posed to check against at the end of the workshop. The specific needs of developing bilingual pupils will need to be highlighted, but issues of language development are relevant to equality in science for* all *children – and particularly working class and Afro-Caribbean pupils who bring 'linguistic diversity' to the classroom as much as do developing bilingual pupils. For further discussion of these issues, see the relevant section in the handbook accompanying this INSET manual.*

## ACTIVITIES
### Stage 1
Participants provided with a set of "Language and learning in science" cards, one set per group of three or four.

## TASK
To discuss a range of viewpoints about language and learning in science.

**1** Facilitator to pose the question "Why is it important to consider language and learning for equality?" on O.H.P. provided. Participants write down, individually, their current ideas and keep for later.    **5 minutes**

*Stage 1: the activities in stage 1 are intended to engage the participants on two levels. In 1) and 2) teachers are asked to formulate their own statements and to consider a variety of other views on language and learning in science which may challenge their own perceptions and practice.*

**2** The statements were made by teachers considering the question "Why do you think language might be important for pupils learning science?" Groups to read and discuss each statement and to decide whether they agree, disagree are aren't sure about each. The blanks can be used to write additional statements of their own.
**20 minutes**

*Activity 2) uses a collaborative discussion process which, in itself, enhances language development and can be usefully adapted for classroom use. Some colleagues may be considering some issues (particularly regarding developing bilingual pupils) for the first time, and sensitive grouping and intervention strategies should be considered.*

### Stage 2
Participants provided with newspaper and sticky tape per group of three or four, one "Purposes of talk" checklist sheet per person and one set of classroom activity sheets per person.

*Stage 2: the activities in stage 2 are practical activities which might be done in any classroom and which involve a high degree of purposeful language use.*

**TASK**

To use examples of classroom activities as the basis for analysing language use and the implications for equality.

**3** Groups asked to construct a freestanding 'chair' from newspaper to support a 2 kg weight or object. One person per group acts as an observor to listen to the language used and to analyse the function/purpose of it, using the checklist provided. Observer reports observations and group briefly discusses these.

**20 minutes**

**4** Groups do and/or discuss one or more classroom-focussed activity from those provided (or others similar):

**a** examples of pupils' writing;

**b** breathing system;

**c** thinking about hotness.

Once again, the checklist can be used to discuss language use and purpose. **25 minutes**

**Stage 3**

**TASK**

To reconsider the initial question posed in the light of activities done.

**5** In groups, participants brainstorm their responses to the initial question for around five minutes, then report back the whole group. Facilitator brings session together using the OHP on "Some principles".

**20 minutes**

*The use of an observer in 3) should by no way inhibit other colleagues from making their own observations about this, or the subsequent activities. The three classroom activity sets are provided for use – although other appropriate language-based activities can be used.*

*Stage 3: it is important that the facilitator brings the session together by re-posing the initial question and asking colleagues to reconsider their initial responses. The checklist sheet and "Some principles" sheet can also be provided as handouts.*

**EVALUATION**

It is important that evaluation takes place after each workshop. It can take place on an individual basis or in small groups. Guidance notes, suggested approaches and a sample evaluation sheet can be found in Appendix 3 of this manual.

*Acknowledgement: Activities and materials on "Thinking about hotness" and the "Breathing system" from* Issues in Science Education: Developing an Anti-Racist Approach, An Inservice discussion pack, *by Pauline Hoyle, 1987.*

*Samples of children's writing, with thanks, from Sir Thomas Aloney Primary School and De Beauvoir Infants' School, Hackney.*

# Assessment

## PURPOSE

• to share, and raise awareness of, strategies of promoting justice and equality in assessment;
• to highlight principles of equality in the issues of assessment.

## RESOURCES

O.H.P./handout, page 101; task and issues sheet, page 102; scenarios, pages 103–104; pupils' profiles, pages 105–106. Paper, pens, flipchart, O.H.P.

**Time: 75 minutes**

## PROCEDURE

Facilitator should introduce the session by stating the purpose and expected duration, and by providing some ideas of activities involved.

## ACTIVITIES

Participants work in groups and are given one copy of "Principles of good assessment" sheet per person, and one set of scenario, profile and task sheets per group of three or four.

## TASK

To consider and apply principles of good assessment and of equality to classroom scenarios and pupils' needs.

**1** Brief presentation by facilitator of "Principles of good assessment" on O.H.P. Participants should be asked if any principles have been missed out – these are then added to the slide. **10 minutes**

**2** Groups to discuss and analyse one scenario as instructed on the task sheet: "Discuss the scenario and decide which principles of good assessment are being addressed in each". Groups can do one more if time allows. **15 minutes**

**3** Groups to work on improving their selected scenario by considering the pupil profiles and issues list provided. Participants should try to ensure that the assessment scenario provides equality of access for the pupils profiled: "How could you improve the scenario(s) to take account of the principles not addressed?" **20 minutes**

**4** Group reporters feedback to whole group, facilitator brings out common strands on flipchart or O.H.P., general discussion of issues. **20 minutes**

## NOTES FOR FACILITATORS

*This workshop is clearly structured around the support materials provided. The workshop starts by looking at general principles of good practice in assessment and aims to show that such good principles are consistent with issues of equality, and that the individual needs of pupils will affect both access to assessment and its outcomes.*

*Activity 1 should not take more than around five minutes, but establishes the ownership of the group of the 'principles' – hence the request that they add any that have been missed out. The workshop does assume, however, that participants are familiar with good practice principles in assessment. The sheet provided acts as a reference point throughout the workshop and as a handout.*

*Activities 2 & 3 are flexible in both time and in the materials used. Facilitators may be able to provide their own scenarios and pupils' profiles which relate better to the experience of the participants. It is suggested that each group selects one scenario to focus on, but time may be given to analyse more if required. Groups should be asked to read the task closely and to be familiar with the "Issues list" provided, which highlights factors in assessment practice which have equal opportunities implications. The pupils' profiles are not age specific and can be used with any scenario. These are designed to be used as 'checks'; the ideal assessment scenario will be one in which all the pupils have equality of access, and the full opportunity to show what they "know, understand and can do". Facilitators should rotate around the groups taking notes and listening to participants.*

*In the feedback Activity 4, use some form of central note taking, eg. O.HP. or flipchart to draw out the main points. Concentrate on common strands, but also note any major areas of debate/disagreement.*

*Participants may need structured time at the end to reflect individually or in pairs on the issues raised in terms of their own classroom practice. Action planning is suggested (see also the "Action planning" workshop in the "Policy development and review" section) but other forms of reflection may be appropriate. It is suggested, however, that participants are encouraged to make some written response/points for action.*

**5** Individual task reflecting on issues in terms of their own classroom practice and experience: "Outline the implications and action for you, your department and/or your school of the issues raised. Identify two key areas you will work on in the next term/year", etc.

**10 minutes**

---

**EVALUATION**

It is important that evaluation takes place after each workshop. It can take place on an individual basis or in small groups. Guidance notes, suggested approaches and a sample evaluation sheet can be found in Appendix 3 of this manual.

---

# Groupings in the classroom

## PURPOSE

To explore the implications for equality of opportunity and access to the curriculum of how pupils/students are grouped in the classroom.

## RESOURCES

Task and contexts, pages 107–109; O.H.P., page 110. Paper, pens, flipchart O.H.P.

**Time: 80 minutes.**

## PROCEDURE

Facilitator should introduce the session by stating the purpose and expected duration, and by providing some ideas of activities involved.

## NOTES FOR FACILITATORS

*This workshop uses seemingly straightforward processes and contexts to stimulate discussion on quite subtle and complex issues. The contexts provided cover a range of situations and the facilitator should select the five/six most appropriate to the group worked with – each group should be given enough cards for one context for each participant. In mixed groups, a random selection of the cards should ensure that positive discussion takes place between colleagues in different phases of education. Where participants are all from the same phase and/or school, facilitators may wish to be more selective, or to write additional contexts or adapt those provided.*

## ACTIVITIES

Each group of five or six is provided with a set of context cards.

**1** Group members take it in turns to read out one context card. The reader then gives a response, i.e. says what s/he would do in the situation listed. The other members of the group discuss each context giving their ideas and responses. The main points are to be noted down. **30 minutes**

*In activity 1, it is important that each group member has a chance to read out and respond to his/her context. Discussion on each card should, therefore, be limited to around five minutes. The facilitator may wish to time this precisely so that each group moves on to the next card at the same signal.*

**2** Groups asked to select one card that they find particularly challenging or interesting, and to consider the question "What are the implications in this situation for equality of opportunity and access for the pupil(s)/student(s) concerned?" Notes to be prepared for report back. **15 minutes**

*In activity 2, discussion focusses on one card and will be more wide ranging and in-depth. participants should be urged, however, to stick to the task provided; that is, to provide a group response to the question posed.*

**3** Each group reports back on their conclusions and discussions. Facilitator notes down main points on flipchart and leads group discussion about general implications for equality of grouping pupils/students in the classroom. Asks question "Can we make a statement of principle which would guide us in the fair grouping of pupils/students to enable access and achievement for all?" **30 minutes**

*In activity 3, reporting back should be done initially without comment from other groups. The facilitator should indicate when questions/comments are welcome (e.g. at the end of each report, or at the end of all the reports). Enough time should be allowed for the discussion on the question – which can be put up on an O.H.P. for reference.*

**4** Each participant writes an individual statement in response to the question posed in 3 above. **5 minutes**

### EVALUATION

It is important that evaluation takes place after each workshop. It can take place on an individual basis or in small groups. Guidance notes, suggested approaches and a sample evaluation sheet can be found in Appendix 3 of this manual.

# Images in science

## PURPOSE

Through the use of photographs:
- to enable teachers to challenge preconceptions regarding science/scientists and people in other countries;
- to show positive images of people around the world involved in scientific activities involving sophisticated knowledge and processes;
- to explore how photographs might be used in classrooms to explore issues in science.

## RESOURCES

Photo notes, page 111; photos, pages 112–115; photo cropping templates, pages 116–117; O.H.P. 1 and 2, pages 118–119; handout, page 120; handout, pages 121–123. Paper, pens, flipchart, sticky tape, card, O.H.P.

**Time: 120 minutes**

## PROCEDURE

Facilitator should introduce the session by stating the purpose and expected duration, and by providing some ideas of activities involved.

## ACTIVITIES

### Stage 1

Facilitator provides photo and cropping cards (see notes); pins set of photos around the room.

## TASK

To use the photo activities to explore images and preconceptions.

**1** In pairs or small groups, the photo provided is covered to leave a small area visible. Facilitator asks participants to discuss what they feel the photo is of, what it is about or what is happening. Record views briefly. After five minutes' discussion, the first cover is removed to reveal more of the photo. The discussion is repeated, and so on until the whole photo is revealed. At this stage participants discuss their original impressions, and compare with the image in the photo. The facilitator to pose question "What does this suggest about our preconceptions and ideas about other people/places, etc." **20 minutes**

**2** All photos are pinned around the room. Individuals or pairs wander round and look at photos. Facilitator asks them to:
- look for the science in the photos;
- choose a photo that they like best or find most interesting, or would like to find out more about. These questions to be discussed with partners or with colleagues who may be looking at the same photo. **20 minutes**

## NOTES FOR FACILITATORS

*The workshop has been designed in two distinct stages. The first is intended for teachers to challenge their own preconceptions regarding images of people and activities from around the world. The second is to explore, more directly, classroom use. In both stages, however, techniques are used which can be used in classrooms and these are covered, together with a rationale, on the handout sheet provided.*

*In both stages preparation by the facilitator is important. In Stage 1, Activity 1, facilitators should choose, and copy, one of the photos provided (a good photocopy should be adequate). Photos 3 and 5 are suggested, and the cropping cards provided are designed for these photos. However, other photos can be used with new cropping templates designed by the facilitator. There should be two to three stages before the whole photo is revealed; it is suggested that the templates are laid one on top of the other on the copy of the photo, with the first on top. Each should then be taped or stapled at the edge so it can be removed separately. Participants should have around five minutes for each stage and the facilitator should not pose the final question until participants have revealed the whole photo.*

*In Activities 2 and 3, individuals or pairs can perform the 'choosing task'. The discussion points are contained on an O.H.P. original which can be displayed during the 'walk-about', if required. When providing information on the photos, either give out copies of the sheet to each participant, or verbally describe them. It may be useful to photocopy the photos on 0to O.H.P. slides to talk through.*

**3** Individuals or pairs feed back on their choice of photo and how they have chosen it; pointing out the science in the photo. Facilitator gives out information on each photo and asks "What do you think now? Does the information surprise you?"
The whole group proceeds to discuss all the photos in the light of the information given. **20 minutes**

## Stage 2
Facilitator provides sets of photos and examples taken from the handout "Some ways of using photographs".

*In Stage 2, Activity 4, the facilitator needs to have read the background sheet on "Why use photographs?" prior to the workshop. The O.H.P. original 2 simply summarises the main points of this paper.*

## TASK
To utilise the photo sets to explore classroom use.

**4** Facilitator asks participants "Now you know what the photos are about, how and why might you use them in the classroom?" Brainstorm activity and facilitator records brainstorm onto O.H.P. or flipchart.
**5 minutes**

**5** Facilitator introduces background information on using photographs with pupils using O.H.P. original provided and handout notes. **5 minutes**

**6** Small groups are given sets of photos and activities. Participants are asked to try activities as if they were pupils/students bearing in mind how they might respond. Facilitator asks them to consider how such activities could support science being performed. **20 minutes**

*During Activity 6, groups need to be given copies of the handout "Some ways of using photographs", or a copy of one or more of the techniques/activities described. They should try these out as if they were a group of pupils/students (one group member may like to take the teacher's role) and stress that they should note how they feel their pupils/students might respond.*

**7** Small groups asked to discuss how schemes of work could arise from the photographs and/or how the photographs might fit into current schemes of work. Take notes for report back. **20 minutes**

*Activity 7 is a flexible curriculum planning exercise in which participants are asked to consider how the photo activities might be used to stimulate new schemes of science work and how they might fit into existing schemes. Groups should take brief notes on these issues for report back.*

**8** Groups briefly report back ideas to whole group and discuss these. Facilitator refers back to original brainstorm list and the points covered from O.H.P. original in 5 above. **10 minutes**

*In the final plenary discussion reporting back is the central activity, but facilitators might like to refer to the the original brainstorm sheet and/or the O.H.P. original "Why use photographs?" to provide a framework for discussion.*

*This workshop is closely related to the "Science themes" and "Science systems" workshops in this section.*

---

**EVALUATION**
It is important that evaluation takes place after each workshop. It can take place on an individual basis or in small groups. Guidance notes, suggested approaches and a sample evaluation sheet can be found in Appendix 3 of this manual.

# Science themes

## PURPOSE
- to encourage cross-curricular thinking around science-based units of work;
- to explore the assertion that:
  - introducing global dimensions and issues can make the science content more relevant for students;
  - science taught within a more holistic framework can increase student interest in the science itself.

## RESOURCES
Task sheets, pages 124–125. Paper, pens, flipchart.

## Time : 60 minutes

## PROCEDURE
Facilitator should introduce the session by stating the purpose and expected duration, and by providing some ideas of activities involved.

## ACTIVITIES

## TASK
To use a *cola can* as a stimulus for thinking about how to plan a cross-curricular scheme of work.

**1** Hand out task sheet 1 to groups of three or four. Groups brainstorm responses around the task question – '' What questions would you pose, or what issues would you explore, in the classroom to make the can the centre of a cross-curricular scheme of work which:
  – includes practical investigations in science;
  – addresses equality and justice issues;
  – uses global contexts?''
Notes taken on sheet or separate paper.  **10 minutes**

**2** Groups feedback to whole group reading their list of questions/issues. No discussion to take place at this stage.  **10 minutes**

**3** Hand out tasksheet 2. Groups are to discuss this, adding further questions and discussing science opportunities and the advantages and disadvantages of such an approach.  **20 minutes**

**4** Whole group feedback and discussion. Each small group reports back on their collective views on this approach and facilitator leads discussion and takes notes on main points emerging.  **20 minutes**

## NOTES FOR FACILITATORS
*It should be stressed that this workshop is not intended to result in detailed curriculum planning at this stage – rather to raise issues regarding the viability of using such an approach to promote a global/equality and justice approach to a science-based topic. The* cola can *is just one example of an artefact which could be used as the centre-piece for discussion by participants (or indeed by pupils in the classroom). Other packaged products such as fruit (e.g. bananas) and other familiar, manufactured artefacts, etc. may serve this purpose equally well. There are many cross-curricular resources which use this approach to discuss issues, e.g.* World Studies 8-13 *materials, Greenlight Publications, and development agency materials (Oxfam, etc.) as well as work by teachers such as Patrick Hazelwood who has highlighted global contexts for teaching chemistry. The workshop relates closely to the ''Global perspectives : ''Images'' and ''Science systems'' workshops in this section and it is suggested that these are used in conjunction with each other, starting with the ''Images'' workshop.*

*When doing the task in activity 1, it may be useful to have access to a checklist for addressing equality and justice issues in the classroom. Such an aide-memoire can be found on pages 135 and 136 (supporting the ''National Curriculum'' workshop in this section).*

## EVALUATION
It is important that evaluation takes place after each workshop. It can take place on an individual basis or in small groups. Guidance notes, suggested approaches and a sample evaluation sheet can be found in Appendix 3 of this manual.

# Science systems

## PURPOSE

• to look at two agricultural systems and explore the impact of these on people and the environment;
• to look at the science in each system and to begin to think about, and explore, the underlying values;
• to explore the view that 'reductionist' (Western) science often results in environmental degredation and increased poverty when applied in 'Third World' countries;

## RESOURCES

Task sheet, page 126; Systems diagrams, pages 127–128; O.H.P., page 129; handout, pages 130–131. Paper, pens, flipchart, O.H.P.

**Time : 75 minutes**

## PROCEDURE

Facilitator should introduce the session by stating the purpose and expected duration, and by providing some ideas of activities involved.

## ACTIVITIES

Participants are provided with two systems diagrams, one set per pair.

## TASK

To discuss and analyse the two diagrams and consider the implications of these for science and teaching science.

**1** Pairs study the two systems diagrams and discuss them. Facilitator poses question "What do you think the two systems mean?". After 5–10 minutes, give out task which asks pairs to look at the science in the two systems. Discuss around questions on sheet.
**20 minutes**

**2** Two pairs join together and, in turn, share with the other pair what conclusions they came to and what questions they would like answered regarding the diagrams. Questions to be noted.　**15 minutes**

**3** Facilitator gives out copies of "Green revolution" handout; participants read and individually relate it to the diagrams.　**10 minutes**

**4** Whole group discusses the two systems in the light of this information. Facilitator asks if any questions remain, encourages other participants to answer them and tries to draw out points in discussion using OHP original.　**20 minutes**

## NOTES FOR FACILITATORS

*This workshop relates more generally to perspectives and contexts which might be useful when teachers are considering planning science schemes of work; but also asks teachers to explore further their own notions of science and what science is for. Because of the specific content of the workshop the facilitator should ensure that they are familiar with the background information on the "Green revolution" provided.*

*The two systems themselves can be summarised as below:*

*System 1 describes a 'reductionist' model in which the factory-bred seed is at the centre of the system. Everything is designed to sustain the seed in artificial conditions to produce high yield. However to grow effectively and produce the high yield, the seed requires extra 'scientifically'-produced support which costs money which has to be raised from selling the resultant crops. The process is therefore a linear one in which there is a start point and an end point and which must be re-started, with new seeds (which do not reproduce), each season. It may be scientific, but does it work?*

*System 2 describes a 'sustainable' system which sees the process as cyclical and in which each process supports the next. Fertilizers are natural coming from the cattle which plough the field. The seeds retained from last year crop produce a harvest which feeds humans, can be sold and the by-products of which feed the cattle. Seeds are then retained for the next planting and so on. The cattle also have a cyclical relationship with the crops and people which is, once again, sustainable and reproduces itself. No expensive high-tech products are involved – but is it scientific?*

**5** Individual reflection – each participant is asked to write one or two sentences in response to the question, "Do you think that taking into account the existence and values of the two systems could lead to a more balanced view of science in the classroom?"

**10 minutes**

(If required these reflections could be shared in a final short report back or collected/collated by facilitator.)

---

**EVALUATION**

It is important that evaluation takes place after each workshop. It can take place on an individual basis or in small groups. Guidance notes, suggested approaches and a sample evaluation sheet can be found in Appendix 3 of this manual.

---

*The nature of the workshop is such that the participants, in Activities 1 and 2 are acting as 'detectives' trying to work out what the systems might mean. It is important, therefore that the facilitator is not drawn into discussion or answering questions until after this stage. In the plenery session in Activity 4, the facilitator leads the whole group discussion in the light of previous activities. Points that should be drawn out are included on the O.H.P. original provided.*

# National Curriculum

## PURPOSE
To investigate opportunities that exist to promote principles of equality and justice through the National Curriculum by:
   - exploring possible links between National Curriculum programmes of study, relevant attainment targets and principles of equality;
   - exploring strategies for translating such links into schemes of work.

## RESOURCES
Chart blank, page 132; Charts O.H.P. 1 and 2, pages 133–134; task and principles sheet, pages 135–136. Paper, pens, flipchart, O.H.P. National Curriculum documents (or equivalent) for science, cross-curricular and other subject areas.

**Time : 70 minutes**

## PROCEDURE
Facilitator should introduce the session by stating the purpose and expected duration, and by providing some ideas of activities involved.

## ACTIVITIES

## TASK
To analyse current units and schemes of work against equality and justice/cross curricular criteria.

## NOTES FOR FACILITATORS
*This workshop is designed to relate directly to the National Curriculum for science as currently defined – but the procedures could be adapted for analysing other Curricular models (eg. other regional or national curricula) or for particular published schemes. Whatever model forms the basis of this workshop, the common aim is to explore ways in which teachers can adapt, change and modify their existing schemes and units of work to reflect equality and justice principles. The other exemplars and scenarios found in other workshops and in the handbook accompanying this manual may also provide useful material. It should be stressed however that the National Curriculum is not overtly anti-racist and simply adding on multicultural elements to exiting schemes of work is in no way an adequate response. Having made connections between National Curriculum and equality and justice principles, teachers should apply the principles found in this, and other, workshops more rigorously when reviewing their science curriculum.*

### Stage 1
**1** Facilitator completes a partially-filled chart on O.H.P. with participants, relating a topic to activities, equality issues and then to attainment target statements and levels. Briefly discuss this exercise demonstrating how to identify activities which may promote equality and justice in the classroom through the choice of context, content and and/or processes (referring to the prompt sheet if required).

*In activities 1 and 2, the chart used is a simple model for mapping the relevant content, processes, principles and issues. Schools may have their own mapping models which are more appropriate – these can be used with the prompt sheets as described. It is assumed that participants will have an understanding of the science National Curriculum. However, copies of relevant documents (and those of other subject orders, etc.) will be needed for specific reference.*

**2** In pairs or individually participants to choose a unit of work they are currently teaching and fill in a blank chart as in 1) above.

### Stage 2
**3** Facilitator poses question on workshop card "How could your existing schemes of work, already in place for the topic chosen, be modified in the light of equality and justice issues (as listed on the principles sheet)?"

*Approaches to 1, 2 and 3 may also differ depending on the phase of education the participants work in. Primary colleagues may be more familiar with this type of mapping exercise, and schemes of work used in 1 and 2 will necessarily be cross-curricular. Secondary colleagues may be used to working more directly from the science programmes of study. This has implications for grouping and reporting back if there is a mixed group of teachers taking part. For clarity, teachers may also wish to focus on a particular key stage in their discussions - although some may wish to*

**4** Return to plenary group and facilitator asks for any useful feedback. This can be recorded or charts collected and re-circulated (see notes).

---

**EVALUATION**

It is important that evaluation takes place after each workshop. It can take place on an individual basis or in small groups. Guidance notes, suggested approaches and a sample evaluation sheet can be found in Appendix 3 of this manual.

---

*explore progression issues. Facilitators should be sensitive to the needs of the group and plan accordingly.*

*The two example provided to illustrate the process are: "Bimwili and the Zimwi", a key stage 1 topic based around the story of that name and "World energy resources", a key stage 4 theme. The key stage 1 theme was taken from the chapter in the handbook on "Early years and key stage 1". The key stage 4 theme was suggested by an edition of GARSP (Gloucestershire anti-racist science project). The theme chosen (with relevant programme of study references) appears in the central box. Up to four relevant activities that could promote equality in its widest sense are then inserted in the boxes available with the equality issues or impliations clearly noted. It should be stressed that it is not always necessary to have four, although we recommend no more than four. In the examples given, only one or two have been completed in detail to illustrate the process; the facilitator is encouraged to discuss further examples on this theme with the participants before proceeding to activity 2. Because participants will need to have an awareness of some of the opportunities and issues, it is recommended that this workshop comes at the end of the "Curriculum Issues" section.*

**STAGE 2: ACTIVITIES 5 & 6**           **TASK**

You have been provided with one or more case studies. In groups of three or four discuss the following questions with relation to the profiles provided.

**1** What strategies could you use to draw out the experiences from pupils who have a diverse range of cultural and life experiences? How would you have ensured that the case study pupils' experiences were shared with you and the class?

**2** How could you build upon the experiences of the case study pupils in a positive way?

**3** Does this activity suggest that you need to change your current practice in any way? If so how?

**4** Could you construct a checklist to help colleagues plan for drawing on pupils' experiences?

**Possible inclusions in a checklist for drawing on pupils' experiences**

• How are topic starting points chosen? What are the criteria? What is the pupil involvement?

• How flexible is the topic structure to include pupils' ideas?

• How does the 'ethos' of the classroom encourage and support individual contributions from pupils?

• Are pupils' backgrounds celebrated through displays, reference materials, artefacts, etc?

• Are parents and other members of the community invited in, if they have a relevant contribution to make?

# Case studies

---

### NADIRA

Nadira is thirteen years old and has been studying in a British secondary school for two years. Her early childhood was spent in north-east Pakistan where she completed her primary education. Nadira is a capable pupil, but reserved and self conscious about her ability to communicate in English. She has many fond memories of her life in rural Pakistan; these are not memories she often shares with her classmates however.

Recently Nadira was silently reminiscing to herself in her science lesson. For some reason she recollected how, at a certain time each year, all the grandmothers in her village would wander off in the direction of the mountains. They would be gone for a few days but would eventually return with sacks full of rock salt. The science teacher had been explaining about rock salt, so Nadira speculated to herself that the grandmothers must have somehow found a seam of rock salt in the mountains. She then tried to remember what they did to it to get it ready for cooking with, but she was distracted by the teacher telling everyone to go and get the equipment for the next practical.

---

### LUCY

Lucy is six years old. She was born in a small town in Ghana, West Africa. She moved to Britain when she was five-and-a-half years old. While she was growing up in Ghana she was always at her mother's side, learning through play and trying to be helpful with the daily chores. She used to enjoy going to market on the bus, even though the bus stop was a long way from home. She remembers how her mother used to carry nearly all the shopping home balanced on her head. Not *all* the shopping though, because Lucy used to carry the pineapple on her head.

Recently when she was going home from school with her mother, Lucy walked along with her sandwich box on her head and pretended she was going home from market. She tried to get her mum to carry her shopping on her head but she wouldn't join in; she said the plastic bag was too floppy.

---

## TARIQ

Tariq is ten years old, he was born in Bangladesh but came to Britain when he was a baby and can't remember anything of the country he was born in. He feels he knows it wel,l though, because his parents, grandparents and older brother and sister often talk about the farm they used to live on. Tariq's father is very good at telling stories about life in Bangladesh. Tariq particularly likes to hear about how his father used to grow sugar cane that grew as tall and thick as a forest and how the leaves could cut your skin easier than a knife. Tariq's father explains how they grew the sugar cane from small pieces of stem. Tariq often wonders if the sugar in the greengrocers could grow in the same way and, if so, how it is processed to look like it does in the shop.

## PARMINDER

Parminder is sixteen years old, studying for his G.C.S.E.s. He was born and bred in Britain but has occasionally visited his relatives who live in the Punjab area of India. He has fond memories of his trips to India, but tends not to mention them in school, partly because the opportunity seldom arises, and partly because he feels there are too many negative images associated with rural India; past experiences tell him that his pride and sensibilities might get knocked. The other day, in a microbiology lesson, the biology teacher got on her hobby-horse about how modern people were polluting the environment with sewage. Parminder, enthusiastically joined in and explained how his farming relatives in India used bio-digesters to convert human sewage into cooking gas and a crop fertilizer. Unfortunately, the bell went just as Parminder started his explanation; he now has to wait and hope that the teacher will be able to explore the issues and the technology in the next lesson.

## BETHAN

Bethan is fourteen years old, she has lived all her life in a small Welsh town. She loves visiting her great grandmother who lives nearby because she is a wonderful storyteller and loves reflecting on her life. Bethan is fascinated by the comparisons her great gran makes between life now, and when she was a girl many years ago. For instance, Bethan's great gran remembers a time when you couldn't buy all sorts of bottles and boxes of cleaners and detergents to clean anything and everything – even if they could have been afforded. She remembers that when the kitchen table needed cleaning after preparing greasy, fatty meat, she would scrub it with white ash from the fireplace. Bethan wondered if her science teacher would know why.

## JULIE

Julie is ten years old and was born in Britain, although her parents originally come from Jamaica. Her parents are both active in local Afro-Caribbean organisations, and Julie attends a Saturday school run by the community, as well as her junior school. At Saturday school she hears stories about the achievements of black people in history and the links that black people all over the world have with Africa. One day the teacher tells of the Dogon people of Mali, who have been studying and charting the stars and planets for many centuries. She learns that the ancient Dogons knew about distant stars which were not charted by Western scientists until modern times. At school her class is doing a topic on "The Earth in Space", and have been using a telescope and finding out how it works. She is very excited about the Dogon story and wants to tell the teacher about how these people charted the stars and planets without any modern telescopes. She hopes that her teacher will be interested and will help her find out more about it.

# Why teach science? - some viewpoints

"The scientific area of learning and experience is concerned with increasing pupils' knowledge and understanding of the natural world and the world as modified by human beings, and with developing skills and competencies associated with science as a process of enquiry…"

**The Curriculum from 5-16, Curriculum Matters 2, 1985, Para. 71**

"Scientific education involves a number of valuable processes which, although they are characterstic of the way in which the scientist works, can also be fostered in other subjects."

**The Curriculum from 5-16, Curriculum Matters 2, 1985, Para. 76**

"Science, in it various forms, represents a rational way of organising knowledge and explaining phenomena which contribute significantly to the cultural and intellectual development of society. Science and technology also contribute powerfully to the generation of wealth in society, and it is therefore important that schools should provide access to a coherent range of ideas if young people are to develop an awareness of the inter-relationship between science, technology and society. Young children develop these ideas from their immediate environment and this lays the foundation for a deepening understanding of the world."

**Primary Support Papers, Northamptonshire L.E.A., 1987, section 14**

"Schools have an important role to play in helping children to understand the world they live in, and in preparing them for adult life and work. We are mindful of the value of our task in helping to equip these citizens of the next century with an education which should stand them in good stead in a world that will be very different from our own. We believe that science has an essential contribution to make in the following ways:

1  Understanding scientific ideas…
2  Developing scientific methods of investigation…
3  Relating science to other areas of knowledge…
4  Understanding the contribution science makes to society…
5  Recognising the contribution science education makes to personal development
6  Appreciating the nature of scientific knowledge."

**Science for Ages 5-16, National Curriculum Proposals, 1988, 2.3**

"As in other areas of the curriculum good science teaching stimulates the children's curiosity, widens their interests and develops positive attitudes to learning. It fosters attitudes which are important to the process of scientific enquiry and which are of wider application and value; for example, perseverance, open-mindedness, respect for evidence, readiness to reflect critically and respect for living things and the environment. In much of the best work, the children undertake investigations in small groups. This helps them to develop their ability to co-operate, to communicate, to negotiate and to respect one another's views. In working together they also learn to share ideas and they teach skills to each other."

*The Teaching and Learning of Science,* **Aspects of Primary Education, HMI/DES, 1989, 65**

"Young people are learning about new things and developing skills which, in time, will give them access to further areas of knowledge. Sometimes pupils, working under the direction of their teacher, do actually carry out scientific research. School science is a reflection of science in the "real" world where scientists learn from each other and extend the boundaries of knowledge by research."

*Science Non-statutory Guidance,* **National Curriculum Council, 1989, 3.3**

" In their early experiences of the world, pupils develop ideas which enable them to make sense of the things that happen around them. They bring these informal ideas into the classroom and the aim of science education is to give pupils more explanatory power so that their ideas can become useful concepts."

*Science Non-statutory Guidance,* **National Curriculum Council, 1989, 6.2**

"The processes of science offer unique opportunities for children to explore critically their own viewpoints and those of others…"

*Race, Equality and Science Teaching,* **Discussion document, ASE, 1990, 3.4**

## STAGE 1: ACTIVITIES 1 & 2 TASK

You have been provided with a set of statements made by a group of teachers about developing the curriculum.

The task is for the group to collectively sort the statements into three piles – those you agree with, those you disagree with and those you are not sure about. Alternatively, you can collectively sort them into a diamond with the one you agree with most at the top, and the one you agree with least at the bottom. Use the blank cards to add any statements of your own, or to change statements into ones you agree with.

For the top three statement you agree with, decide how you would recognise how each is being put into practice, and note down your responses. That is, develop criteria by which you could judge whether the principle in the statement has been applied in the classroom.

## STATEMENTS BY TEACHERS

> **1** I think it's important to find out about pupils' ideas and try to build upon them as I go along.

> **2** I know that I am better at some classroom strategies than others, but I try to suggest a range of activities when I plan schemes of work.

> **3** I think it's important to evaluate materials before I use, or buy, them because they've often got lots of prejudice and bias in them.

> **4** I think it's really important to think how to use materials, because sometimes biased materials can be used to bring out points about prejudice and discrimination.

> **5** I think it's really important to include historical and present-day examples of science throughout the world. Then pupils can get the idea that science is not just a modern, Western or European activity.

**6** I think it's really important that science is always put in historical, social, cultural, economic and political contexts so that pupils can see how it fits into their other perceptions of the world.

**7** I think it's important to encourage pupils to have a critical approach when reading books about science. It helps them to assess all materials they come into contact with, and not always believe everything they see in print.

**8** I think it's really important for pupils to understand that people everywhere are scientists and do science – otherwise they get the idea that science is done only by people in white coats in laboratories.

**9** I think it's really important for us, as teachers, to use a whole variety of teaching and learning approaches because not all pupils learn in the same way. It's best to give them as many different opportunities as possible.

**10** I think it's really important for us to remember the role language has in learning, and that there are opportunities for language development in *all* areas of the curriculum. So it's really essential for us to help pupils to learn, talk, read and write better in science.

**11** I think it's very important for pupils to realise, through the science curriculum, how powerful science and scientists have been, particularly in this century, and for them to think carefully about the uses and abuses of science.

**12** It seems to me that teachers too often give a reductionist view of science - always concentrating on bits like cells, organs and molecules, rather than starting with whole structures of systems like the body.

You have been provided with a set of scenarios describing examples of classroom practice. You are going to apply the principles and criteria for curriculum development for equality discussed in Stage 1 to these scenarios.

Read out and discuss each scenario in turn. Decide, for each one, which of the principles and criteria you discussed earlier are being addressed.

Select one scenario you find most interesting and make brief notes on the above task for reporting back.

For this scenario, consider how the teacher and pupils described could further develop the topic or theme so that more of these principles are addressed – or that they are addressed in more depth.

## CLASSROOM SCENARIOS

### SCENARIO 1

A group of students have been studying malaria and the teacher has informed them that the disease is no longer the killer that it once was since the discovery of quinine. The next day, a student comes to class and expresses the view that the teacher is mis-informed. The student had been talking to friends from the Congo who maintained that more people were dying in that country from malaria than any other disease, yet more money was spent on military arms than on medical care. The student stated that Western aid to the Congo is more heavily weighted to military rather than medical needs because of the stategic importantce of the country to the West.

The students continue to discuss this with the teacher and decide to base an assignment on the issue.

## SCENARIO 2

A year 3 class started a topic on electricity by discussing what they already knew, and listing what they wanted to find out about. They started by talking about toys and household gadgets that work with batteries, and by considering the different uses of electricity that are made at home and at school. The pupils then discussed what their lives would be like without electricity and they researched this with their older friends and relations, and by using books at school.

They visited the local museum and learnt when electricity supply and electrical lights were first introduced to houses in Britain. They learnt about the work on filaments of the black scientist, Lewis Latimer, which contributed to the development of the light bulb.

Back at school they explored making series and parallel circuits with batteries and bulbs, and discussed which would be the best arrangement for lighting up a dolls' house.

## SCENARIO 3

Pupils in a year 2 class were studying a topic on cooking. They discussed their favourite foods and talked about cooking utensils. In the home corner they had utensils from throughout the world, which they played with. The teacher then invited the pupils to bring in any herbs and spices used at home to flavour foods. The pupils were asked to find out as much as they could about their herbs and spices for a poster which could be put in the display corner. Over a period of time, pupils observed the herbs and spices closely, sorted them in a variety of ways and considered their similarities and differences. They predicted which herbs or spice would be the easiest to identify through smell and designed a fair test to see if they were correct.

The pupils then cooked using some of the herbs and spices assisted by parents and helpers. This brought negative comments about the smells from some of the pupils, parents and staff and some pupils were reluctant to try out some of the unfamiliar foods. The teacher felt it was vital to address the issues that these activities brought up and to set a positive example about respecting each other, and being open to new things.

## SCENARIO 4

A year 6 group are studying the topic of growth and change. At one stage they focus on the growth and change of their local community. One group of pupils studies the area 150 years ago, another group studies the present time while another considers 150 years in the future. They concentrate on a variety of aspects – jobs and industry, diets, religion, education, family life, etc. Particular attention is paid to green spaces in the area, pressures on the environment by changes in population and land use, and effects on the natural environment. The results of the study lead to action by pupils to create extra habitat space for wildlife within the school grounds. The trends they study help them to predict future life styles that could be more sustainable by the the area and less harmful to the local environment. The project exhibition is so successful that it influences consultation processes by the local council on the future development of the area.

## SCENARIO 5

Some year 10 students are studying microbes. As part of the study they look at the role of microbes in the disposal of sewage. This results in a visit to the local sewage farm. The pupils also study material about India's 1.2 million domestic bio-gas digestors. These convert household waste into fertiliser whilst producing bio-gas, saving 4.24 million tonnes of firewood a year. They also read a report by the BMA which point out that U.K. beaches are so polluted with sewage that only 29 out of 440 of them qualify for the European Community "Blue Flag" for cleanliness.

## SCENARIO 6

Year 11 students have been doing some work on world energy resources. They have considered renewable and non-renewable sources of energy and are moving onto recycling and the implications on world energy resources. They have been given data on energy demands of producing aluminium, uses of aluminium products and the energy involved in recycling aluminium cans. The pupils are asked to work in groups to present different viewpoints for a debate on "The need for aluminium in the 21st century: a question of energy and resources". They are given resources from aluminium companies, recycling companies, Friends of the Earth, Energy Commission, etc.

**SCENARIO 7**

Pupils in year 9 are studying food as a topic and have watched a video about food production in the world. The video includes interviews with various people connected with food production and aid agencies. At one stage in the video a government employee talks about people in India not growing the right food. It then shows a rural scene in which it is suggested that people want to grow cash crops instead of food crops. It shows workers in the field, poorly dressed and bent over the cash crops they are tending, while children in the village are suffering from malnutrition. The workers are being watched over by a well-dressed overseer who holds a rather large stick in his hand and is walking along the field behind the workers.

At the end of the video the pupils talk with the teacher about world food production and the images shown in the video. In particular the pupils mention the unfair treatment of the farmer workers in India. The teacher gets the pupils to form small groups to discuss and produce a role play to show how the video could have portrayed the farm workers dilemma: whether to grow food and have a subsistence-level existence or whether to grow cash crops and hope that they will bring in enough money with which to buy food. In a subsequent drama lesson another teacher works with the pupils on this topic.

**SCENARIO 8**

A group of students were studying a topic on forces and were given the following situation to resolve:-

A village in a very rural part of Iraq needs to raise water 25 metres from a stream to irrigate crops. Large amounts of water need to be raised because, in the rebuilding of the country after the war, it has been decided that this area would be a good place to grow large amounts of edible crops. However in the dry months the stream often dries up and the traditional method of obtaining water from a well using buckets is very slow. The village has been offered an electrical pump but the fuel to drive it is not readily available and replacement parts of the pump are difficult to install.

## SCENARIO 9

Pupils in a year 5 class are involved in a project on transport. They started by surveying the main road for types of transport used, and questioned their families and friends about how they travel around. The pupils debated the advantages and disadvantages of different types of transport, which included arguments about pollution and accidents. Although most of them used either bicycles or buses, they decided that life was much easier for people if they have cars. They discussed things that could be done to improve life for those without cars, and to encourage people to use their cars less.

Some people brought bicycles and examined them to find out how they worked. They studied things like brakes, gears, stopping distances and the tools used to fix them. The class then visited the local bicycle shop and interviewed the mechanic about her job, and what science she needed to know to mend bikes.

## SCENARIO 10

Pupils in a year 7 class are starting work on a force unit. They are asked to work in groups and write down as many sentences as they can in which they've heard the word "force" used. They came up with expressions like "Arsenal are a force to be reckoned with"; "My mum always forces me to go to bed by 9 p.m."; "My uncle says it's dangerous to go sailing in a gale force 9 wind".
Each group is asked to present their sentences to the class. For homework the pupils are asked to draw a title page for their work on forces.

## SCENARIO

Some Year 10 pupils studied microbes. As part of the study they looked at the role of microbes in the disposal of sewage. This resulted in a visit to the local sewage farm. The pupils also studied material about India's 1.2 million domestic bio-gas digestors. These convert householde waste into fertiliser whilst producing bio-gas, saving 4.24 million tonnes of firewood a year. They also read a report by the BMA which pointed out that UK. beaches are so polluted with sewage that only 29 out of 440 of them qualify for the European Community "Blue Flag" for cleanliness.

At the end of one lesson in this study the conversation on the tape took place. A deputy headteacher observed the lesson as part of a review or appraisal procedure, and spent a little time checking out some of the aspects of the lesson in preparation for the review or appraisal meeting the following week.

## TASK

Having listened to the tape and raised issues, your group is to take ownership of one of the issues and discuss it, responding to the following questions:

1 Why is it important to take action?
2 What would you/the group do about it?
3 Have you experienced anything similar?
4 What did you do?
5 How did it work out?

Take notes on your responses for reporting back and appoint a reporter for the plenary session.

# Transcript of conversation

Note: it is intended that the following transcript be taped prior to the workshop session by two colleagues in role, reading the script. For alternative ways of using this see the facilitator's notes.

## SCENARIO

Some Year 10 pupils studied microbes. As part of the study they looked at the role of microbes in the disposal of sewage. This resulted in a visit to the local sewage farm. The pupils also studied material about India's 1.2 million domestic bio-gas digestors. These convert householde waste into fertiliser whilst producing bio-gas, saving 4.24 million tonnes of firewood a year. They also read a report by the BMA which pointed out that UK. beaches are so polluted with sewage that only 29 out of 440 of them qualify for the European Community "Blue Flag" for cleanliness.

At the end of one lesson in this study the conversation on the tape took place. A deputy headteacher (D.H.) observed the lesson as part of a review or appraisal procedure for the teacher (Sue), and spent a little time checking out some of the aspects of the lesson in preparation for the review or appraisal meeting the following week.

## TRANSCRIPT

**D.H.**  OK Sue, how did you find that lesson went?

**Sue**   Well I think it was mostly alright, although I was a bit disappointed at the end when I was trying to pull things together. I was also concerned about the reaction of some of them to the video.

**D.H.**  Yes that was a surprise – did you hear that comment from David?, **"Oh, look there's Abdul's grandma"**[1] and then something about Abdul being even uglier than that?

**Sue**   I didn't hear that but I did find their reaction to the people on the video a bit disconcerting. **They thought the whole thing very primitive**[2]. Shirley's aside about her dad's theory of "them lot will never learn" didn't help either!

**D.H.**  Yes and then Cheryl's stroppiness about, "Why do we have to find out about this in science – what's it to do with us anyway?" just added to the general disquiet. Having said that **most of the Asian girls seem to get on quietly and work well**, don't they – they're never a problem! [3] I tell you, you could do with some of those kids on the video in the class, they'd be real workers and not give you the hassle that some of ours do!  Anyway what about the group work afterwards?

**Sue**   Oh, I was pleased with that, they really did engage with the discussion didn't they? They've got much better at giving each other the chance to speak and there are a good few of them developing chairing skills which is great. The only real problem I've got these days is **Chung - he always gets left out.**[4]

**D.H.**  Yes, mind he is a bit of a loner round school as well isn't he? Do you think it's a language problem? He's still very difficult to understand.

**Sue**   Could be. That's one of the reasons I want to encourage him in a group, it would help his language development.

**D.H.**  I think we'd better draw things to a close for now, just one last thing. You said you weren't happy with the drawing together at the end…?

**Sue**   Yes, that was the thing I was most disappointed with. They seemed to be so tied up with obscene comments about sewage that they **didn't make any connections** about the positive images they'd seen[5] of bio-gas production in India and the negative aspects of sewage in Britain – they just didn't pick it up at all!

**D.H.**  Well, perhaps we can draw on that at your review meeting. I do think, though, that there was a great deal of learning going on in that lesson and I find it very interesting myself, not being a scientist. Anyway we'll pick up some of this next Wednesday, thanks.

# Reference sheet for 'conversation' discussions.

(For use by facilitator in leading discussion)

**QUOTE 1** "Oh look, there's Abdul's grandma…"
**Issue:** Kinds of reactions to images of black people.
**Notes:**
- An example of stereotyping – all Indian people look the same;
- A narrow view of normal or good looking – other groups are ugly;
- Do other groups consider white people as "all looking the same"? What evidence have we for this?
- Why do we view others as all the same? Laziness? Lack of observation skills?
**Reference:** "Race" quotes on handout and O.H.P. originals.

**QUOTE 2** "They thought the whole thing very primitive…"
**Issue:** Perceptions of science and the irrelevance of black images in science.
**Notes:**
- Students' reaction to science was that black people are primitive – this arises from the perception of science in a non-western setting as inferior because of its setting. The perception is supported by, for example, the apparent lack of high tech trappings; people not dressed in white coats.
- Students bring parents' attitudes into the lesson and quote such remarks as evidence. It may be a way of disengaging from uncomfortable ideas which images raise, e.g. sewage washed up on UK beaches.
**Reference:** "Science for people" and "Global perspectives" workshops in this section.

**QUOTE 3** " Most of the Asian girls get on quietly and work well…"
**Issue:** Deputy's appreciation of "hardworking Asians" is stereotyping students' behaviour by ethnicity.
**Notes:**
- Will the expectation of quiet behaviour from one group cause this teacher to deal differently with a noisy incident from an Asian girl?
- Will the perception of Cheryl's "stroppiness" cause this girl's question to be dealt with differently?
- Could pupils be aware of different expectations and behave accordingly, e.g. the quiet student reluctant to question, even when they have the same concerns as other students?
**Reference:** "Groupings" workshop in this section.

..................................................................................

**QUOTE 4** "..Chung - he always gets left out...."
**Issue:** Teacher's perception of the isolated child who can't be understood.
**Notes:**

• To what extent is Chung's learning being affected by being "left out"?

• What kind of support is needed?

• This shows a case of a child being denied access to the curriculum because of a communication difficulty;

• Could the class be organised and resourced in a way that helps Chung to be part of a group?

• How could language support be provided for Chung so that he could participate?

**Reference:** "Language and learning in science" workshop in this section.


**QUOTE 5** "They didn't make any connections…"
**Issue:** Attitudes towards global perspectives.
**Notes:**

• A case of students being unwilling or unable to make connections between science in the U.K. and elsewhere in the world (see also 2 above);

• Science carried out in India is not the same as in the U.K. (or West);

• Viewpoint is "people doing it are not the same as us, then by definition, the science is not relevant!";

• Students unable to see the 'primitiveness' of the UK sewage disposal system;

• Pupils need to see the value of the bio-gas generator as an appropriate piece of science and technology.

**Reference:** "Science for people" and "Global perspectives" workshops in this section.


**KEY QUESTION TO POSE**:

■  WHERE DO THESE ATTITUDES AND IDEAS COME FROM?

...........................................................................................................

## Racism prevents entitlement

By its very nature, racism aims to devalue specific groups of human beings based on the colour of skin and/or cultural and social background. If an entitlement to a balanced and relevant science curriculum is to be taken up by every child, there must be a recognition that, in establishing equality of opportunity, racism will always have a negative effect on children's learning, achievement and attitudes towards others.

## 'Race' is not a valid scientific concept

Far from reflecting an 'objective reality', science has on occasions been used to justify racist practices. The concept of 'human race' is itself an example of this process; pseudo-scientific theories which divided humanity into distinct racial types were used to justify social and political policies in the U.S.A., European colonies and Britain. It is only recently that these theories have been discarded, although references to 'racial types' can still be found in some older school science text books and other sources. The concept of 'human race' has no scientific validity, but is a social and historical concept which all teachers of science have a duty to challenge.

## Teachers should challenge racist attitudes, assumptions and behaviour

The processes of science offer unique opportunities for children to explore critically their own viewpoints and those of others, and teachers of science can help in challenging prejudice directly. Teachers need to recognise and to deal firmly and consistently with all forms of racial abuse; teachers themselves should avoid making stereotypical judgements and expectations of a pupil's performance.

Although good teaching can tackle racism, it is most effective when performed within the context of whole school or department policy. These policies should provide strategies which seek to eliminate all forms of racism and should set clear procedures for dealing with racist incidents…

*(Extracts from* Race, Equality and Science Teaching *– a discussion paper which appears as an appendix to this manual.)*

■ By its very nature, racism aims to devalue specific groups of human beings based on the colour of skin and/or cultural and social background...

■ Racism will always have a negative effect on children's learning, achievement and attitudes towards others...

■ Far from always reflecting an 'objective reality', science has on occasions been used to justify racist practices, the concept of 'human race' is itself an example of this process…

■ The concept of 'human race' has no scientific validity, but is a social and historical concept which all teachers of science have a duty to challenge.

Teaching and learning promotes equality when:

- a variety of strategies is used;

- children's own experience is valued and built on;

- children are enabled to develop autonomy and responsibility for their own learning;

- ideas and assumptions are challenged;

- strategies are collaborative, not competitive;

- control of learning is shared between teachers and pupils.

## ACTIVITY 3              TASK

You have been provided with a set of cartoon 'scenarios' showing different styles of teaching and learning. You discuss all these, but should take responsibility for reporting back to the whole group on one or two cartoons.

Examine your cartoons and consider the following questions:

- What learning is going on?

- Who is learning?

- How is the situation in the cartoon promoting equality?

Take notes and identify a member of your group to report back on your cartoons to the whole group.


## CARTOONS OF TEACHING AND LEARNING

## ACTIVITY 3                                                                    TASK

## ACTIVITY 5                                                      TASK

The following list of teaching and learning approaches is for use in Activity 5, but may be useful for reference throughout the workshop.

In Activity 5, groups of participants are asked to identify which have the potential for promoting equality and why.

## TEACHING AND LEARNING APPROACHES

- drama techniques and structures including role play, simulation, tableaux, hot seating, etc.

- small group discussion

- presentation work: pupil demonstations, posters, report back, etc.

- group interactive tasks

- brainstorming

- puzzles, wordsearches, games

- pupils following a plan

- pupils producing their own plan

- small group investigation

- testing

- observation tasks

- problem solving

- field work

- teacher-directed questioning

- notetaking

- self-supported study

- data search

- DARTS (Directed Activities Related to Text)

- project work

- visits

- dictation

- talk and chalk

- team teaching

- use of video, tape-slides, audio

- use of I.T. for writing, analysis, etc.

# Why do you think language might be important for pupils learning science?

## STAGE I: ACTIVITY 2 TASK

The statements on the cards were made by teachers considering the question:

"Why do you think language might be important for pupils learning science?"

In groups, read and discuss each statement. Decide whether you agree, disagree or aren't sure about each of them.

Use the blanks to add statements of your own.

## STATEMENTS BY TEACHERS

> Pupils learn to think scientifically by being allowed hands-on experience and actually doing investigations.

> If pupils can't communicate then any knowledge they have got is useless.

> Without good English, pupils can only make limited observations.

> Pupils need language to discuss and explain their observations.

> Pupils need to be able to understand what the teacher says and the language that teachers use, if they're to learn any science.

> The language used in most science textbooks is too difficult for most pupils, so it has to be simplified.

## STAGE 1: ACTIVITY 2

If pupils can't speak English, there's no way they can learn any science.

If pupils first talk about their ideas on a scientific topic before they read and write about it, then they are more likely to learn and enjoy science.

Pupils don't read instructions – you have to tell them how to do everything, otherwise they can't do their experiments.

It is best if you can make science 'language-free' because pupils can get on with learning science without becoming confused.

If pupils are to understand science it is important for them to be able to communicate their ideas in whatever ways they can.

All pupils need help to extend their language repertoire so they can communicate in academic science and pass exams.

All pupils, particularly bilingual pupils, eventually need to be taught the 'language of science' and 'the language of exams' so they successfully gain access to the system. This needs to be the end point of teaching, not the beginning.

························································································

The following checklist can be used to analyse the talking that goes on when people in your group are carrying out the task.

Add any extra ideas of your own.

Record the uses. You might like to record how often, or when, people use the different types of talk.

---

**Some purposes of talk**

---

Negotiating and cooperating

Making predictions

Asking questions

Explaining ideas

Reporting to each other

Making suggestions

Repeating ideas

Reviewing

Sequencing ideas

# Children's writing

In groups of three, look at the samples of pupils' writing and consider and discuss the following questions:

**1** What do each of these samples show you about children's learning in science?

**2** How do different forms of writing support children's learning in science?

**3** In what situation(s) could you use each form of writing?

**TRANSCRIPT OF MAX'S WRITING** (next page)

I FOUND A LEAF A LEAF

WITH COLOURS IN THE

VEINS. WHEN I

TURNED IT OVER I SAW

A BEETLE BLACK AND IT HAD BLACK SPOTS.

IT HAD A CONKER

WHICH WAS

SPLIT IN HALF

AND SOMETHING

WAS SPARKLING IN THE LEAF

WHEN I CAME BACK

NOTHING WAS THERE

MAX

I FOU A LEAV A LEAV WTH KLS IN THE VANS. WEAN I IERND IT OVER I SAW A BTL BKA AND IT HETD BKA SPOTS. IT HETD A CONKER WICH WAS SPLIT IN HALF AND SOMETHING WAS SPARKLING IN THE LEAI WEAN I CAM BACK NITHING WAS THERE.

MAX

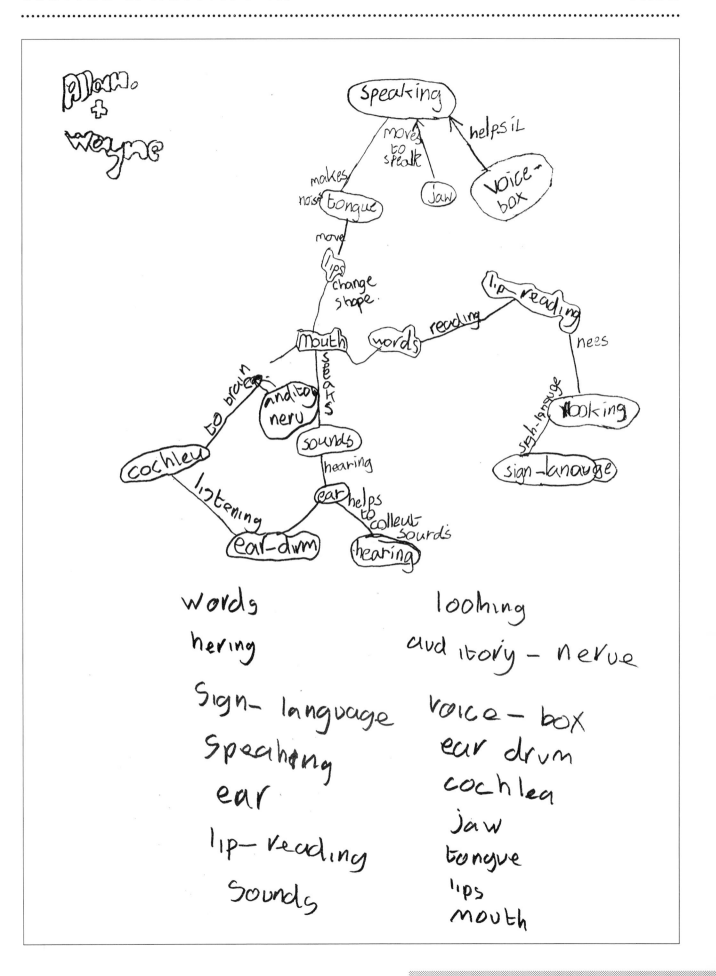

We made cars.

We made cars and we made controls so we could work the cars. We put wires on to the motor then to the controls and then up to the batteries. In the controls you push the paperclip back and it goes so the electricity can go through.

We had problems making it. We tried to fit pieces together. It was hard. We kept on getting mixed up with the wires. It wouldn't work when the wires dropped off.
Gemma.

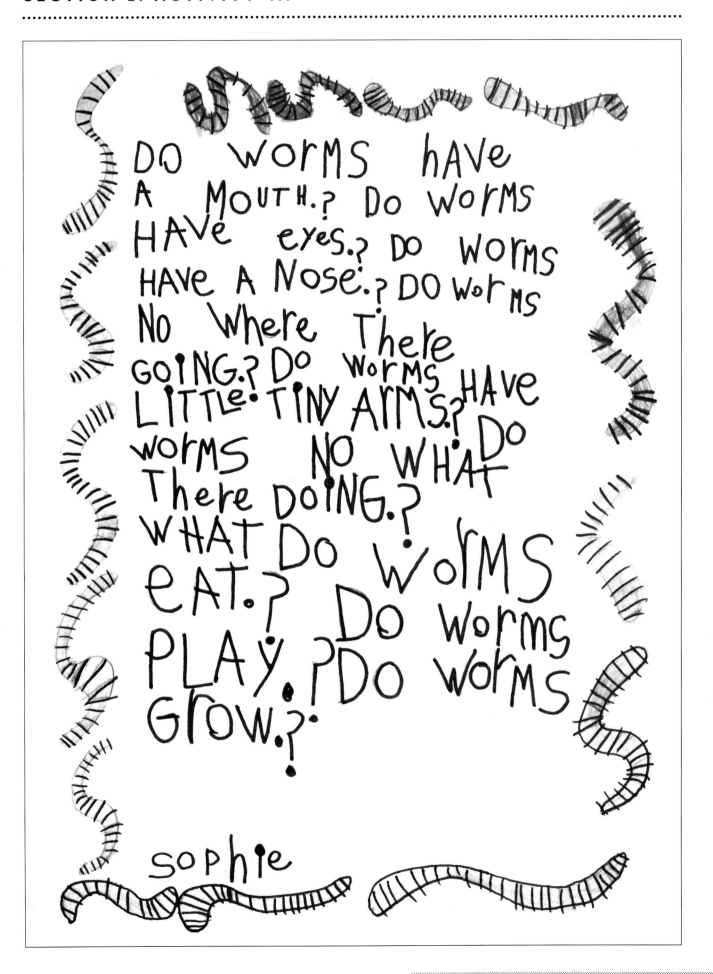

DO WORMS HAVE A MOUTH.? DO WORMS HAVE eyes.? DO WORMS HAVE A NOSe.? DO WorMS NO Where There GOiNG.? DO WORMS LITTLe TiNY ARMS.? HAVE WORMS NO WHAT Do There DOiNG.? WHAT Do WORMS eAT.? Do WORMS PLAY.? DO WORMS GroW.?

sophie

# The breathing system

- Look at the diagram. In your group, share out the cards with the parts and functions of the breathing system.
- Take it in turns to read each card and try to label each part with a card.
- Then try to match each function to the correct part.
- Check your ideas by reading the sheet called "The Breathing System".
- Make any necessary corrections and keep a record of your decisions.

## PARTS

| | | |
|---|---|---|
| Diaphragm | Pleural membranes | Trachea (windpipe) |
| Bronchioles | Ribs | Larynx |
| Nose | Bronchus | Air sacs (made up of alveoli) |

## FUNCTIONS

| | |
|---|---|
| These surround and protect the lungs and heart. | These take the air to all parts of the lungs. |
| This cleans and warms the air as it passes through. | This moves to help with breathing in and out. |
| This transports air from the trachea to the lung. Its hairs collect dust and dirt. | This helps make the sound bigger when air passes through it. |
| This produces a liquid to reduce damage by friction as the lungs rub against the ribs during breathing. | This stays open all the time to allow the air to get from the mouth and nose to the lungs. |

These allow gaseous exchange to take place so that oxygen (O) moves from the air in the alveolus into the blood. At the same time, carbon dioxide ($CO_2$) moves from the blood to the air in the alveolus.

**PARTS**

**FUNCTIONS**
Match with
correct part

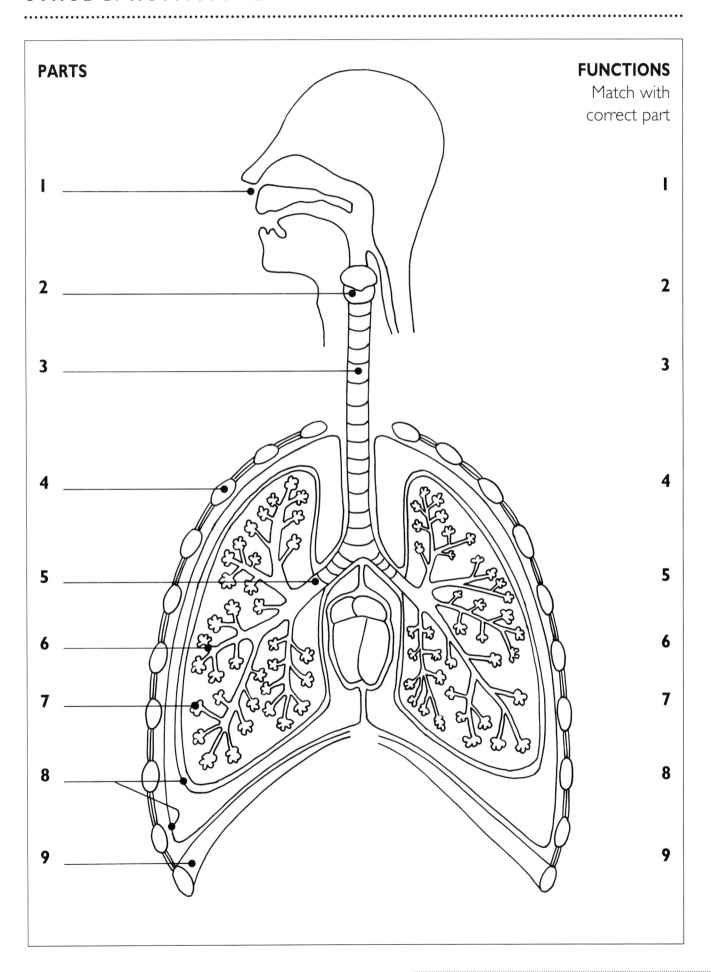

1

2

3

4

5

6

7

8

9

1

2

3

4

5

6

7

8

9

# The breathing system

When we breathe, air can enter the body either through the nose or the mouth. It is better to breathe through your nose because the structure of the nose allows the air to become warm, moist and filtered before it gets to the lungs.

The hairs and mucus in the nose filter the air by trapping bacteria, dirt and dust. There are also lots of blood capillaries inside the nose which help to warm the air as it passes through.

## Down the windpipe
At the back of the nose and throat, the air enters the windpipe or trachea. At the top of the windpipe there is a bulge called the voicebox or larynx. This has cords in it which vibrate as air passes over them. This allows us to talk and make other sounds.

The rest of the windpipe is 12 cm long. It has C-shaped rings of cartilage. These strengthen it, so that it can stay open all the time to let the air pass from the mouth and nose to the lungs. There are also hairs to filter the air.

## Into the lungs
The trachea or windpipe divides into two short tubes. Each tube is called a bronchus, which takes air into the lungs. Like the windpipe, each bronchus has hairs to filter the air, and cartilage rings for support.

Inside the lungs, the bronchus divides into many smaller tubes called bronchioles. The bronchioles take the air to all parts of the lung. At the end of each bronchiole there are many tiny air sacs. Each air sac is made up of thin membranes called alveoli which are surrounded by blood vessels. Each alveolus lets gas exchange take place. This means that the oxygen moves from the air in the alveolus into the blood. At the same time, carbon dioxide moves from the blood to the air in the alveolus.

## Surrounding the lungs
The lungs are covered by a thin, shiny, slippery membrane, or skin. This is called the pleural membrane and it makes a liquid so that the lungs are not damaged if they rub against the rib cage. The rib cage is made of many bones called ribs, which surround and protect the lungs and heart. Under the lungs is a large sheet of muscle called the diaphragm. This stretches across the body and helps in breathing in and out.

This activity reproduced from *Issues in Science Education: Developing an Anti-racist Approach,*
P Hoyle and C Lainé, 1987.

# Thinking about hotness

- Read the statements below which are all about 'hotness'.

- Discuss each statement in your groups.

- Put the statements in order of hotness, with the hottest at the top. Write them on a large sheet of paper.

## STATEMENTS

| | |
|---|---|
| **1** The temperature of a hot bath. | **2** The temperature of a cup of tea. |
| **3** The temperature of the body. | **4** The temperature of the classroom. |
| **5** A hot summer's day in England (25°F 12C). | **6** An average day in the Caribbean (27°F 12C). |
| **7** A cold winter's day in England (2°F 12C). | **8** The temperature of milk that has been in the fridge. |
| **9** The temperature of water from the cold tap. | **10** The temperature of water in a heated swimming pool. |
| **11** The temperature of an 'ice pole'. | **12** The temperature of a blue flame of a bunsen burner. |
| **13** The temperature of a centrally-heated house in an English winter. | **14** The temperature of an air-conditioned house in the rainy season of a tropical country. |

## SOME PRINCIPLES

■ Talk is the basis of all language development;

■ Talking through ideas enables a learner to clarify ideas and develop thinking;

■ The development of critical awareness requires a person to be thinking and to use their thinking skills;

■ Equality is based upon autonomy, which has stemmed from the ability to use language and develop critical awareness;

■ Language and its effect on learning are therefore essential to equality.

# Some principles

"Language is the means of learning throughout the school curriculum and throughout every key stage…It is essential that opportunities are created to develop children's learning through language, about language and as users of language, in all curriculum areas.

"Pupils should:

* experience different contexts for language use;
* achieve success and enjoyment in writing and in responding to books and visual texts;
* reflect on and make explicit their knowledge of how language works;
* draw on their cultural identity;
* work with others;
* become confident and independent in using language;
* ask and answer questions;
* initiate and sustain ideas;
* take part in planning their work;
* evaluate their own and others' work."

***English Non-statutory Guidance,* N.C.C. 1990, A1.1 and A1.7**

"Teachers should accordingly be encouraged to develop whole school policies on language which are sensitive to their local circumstances and which bear in mind principles such as the following:

when children leave school they should have acquired as far as possible:

* a firmly based, but flexible and developing, linguistic and cultural identity;
* an awareness of some of the basic properties of human languages and their role in societies;
* a respect for other languages and cultures, and an understanding of the increasing integration of cultures in society; and
* a willingness and capability to overcome communication barriers."

"We believe that these characteristics are applicable to good practice in primary and secondary schools…

* a very high expectation of success for the learner;

- an 'apprenticeship' approach to acquiring written and oral language, in which the adult represents the 'success' the child seeks and yet offers endless help;
- maximum encouragement and support whilst errors are mastered;
- motivation for the learner to make sense of and acquire control over language and the power which it can have;
- a constant respect for the child's language…

"…the learner needs

- expectation of success;
- the confidence to take risks and make mistakes;
- a willingness to share and to engage;
- the confidence to ask for help;
- an acceptance of the need to readjust,

and the teacher needs

- respect for and interest in the learner's language culture, thought and intentions;
- the ability to recognise growth point, strengths and potential;
- the confidence to maintain breadth, richness and variety, and to match these to the learner's interests and direction (i.e. to stimulate and challenge);
- a sensitive awareness of when to intervene and when to leave alone."

*English for Ages 5 to 16*, **D.E.S./H.M.S.O. June 1989, 2.12 and 3.1**

# PRINCIPLES OF GOOD ASSESSMENT

**Assessment should:**

- influence and inform future teaching and learning;

- show what pupils know, understand and can do;

- measure pupil progress;

- provide feedback to pupils, teachers and parents;

- give pupils a positive sense of achievement and therefore empower them.

**In assessment we need to:**

- use a range of strategies;

- give pupils adequate time and opportunities to show what they can do;

- plan it as part of normal classroom activity;

- share the criteria with pupils;

- present activities in a way which makes them accessible to *all* pupils;

- set activities in a context in which a pupil performs best;

- use contexts which draw upon pupils' ideas and experiences;

- involve a range of contexts and pupils groupings;

- involve pupils in the planning of the activity;

- relate the criteria to the learned objective of the activity.

**1** You have been provided with a set of scenarios and a "Principles of good assessment" sheet. Read through them as a group and then select one (or two) scenarios. Discuss the scenario(s) and decide which principles of good assessment are being addressed.

**2** You have also been provided with a number of pupil profiles. Using these and the 'issues list' below, you are asked to try to improve the scenarios to take account of the principles not addressed. To help you do this, share out the pupil profiles and take on the role of the pupil in considering the issues listed below.

Then make notes on how the group feels the scenario(s) could be improved. The ideal assessment scenario will be one in which all the pupils have equality of access and opportunity to show what they 'know understand and can do'. Select one person in the group to act as the reporter for the plenary session.

## ASSESSMENT ISSUES

Consideration of these issues could help promote and enhance equality in the assessment described in each scenario.

• **method of assessment used,** e.g. observation, written response, self-assessment, questioning, listening to discussions;

• **presentation of the activity,** e.g. language used, format of written materials, time and variety of methods used to introduce activities, visual/audio prompts, opportunities to use pupils' prior ideas or questions;

• **content of the activity** related to real life, pupils' experiences and questions, global issues;

• **climate or setting of the classroom,** e.g. access for pupils to resources, labelling of resources, grouping of pupils, valuing pupils' contributions, pupils respecting each other, listening to each other;

• **expectations of the teacher,** e.g. expecting *all* pupils to achieve, encouraging shy or awkward pupils, distinguishing pupil behaviour from pupil achievement, valuing bilingualism in pupils, encouraging the involvement of pupils with special educational needs and different physical abilities.

# Assessment scenarios

## SCENARIO 1

A class of year 2 pupils were doing some investigations on magnetism. There was a class teacher and a support teacher working with the pupils. The class teacher extracted a group of six pupils to work on magnets. The group was a mixture of bilingual and monolingual pupils.

Each of the six children were supplied with a magnet and they went around the school testing materials for magnetism. The teacher questioned the pupils on why they were doing what they did, and why they were not doing other things. In the nursery there was a tray set out that had everyday objects on it. They had to sort the tray out into things that were magnetic and things that were not magnetic. The teacher asked questions about what was magnetic in the tray. The pupils were encouraged to predict which things were magnetic before they tested them.

## SCENARIO 2

A year 8 class was doing some work on structures and forces. At the beginning of the lesson the teacher explained to the whole class that they were going to examine some types of floor covering that the pupils had brought from home. They were told that they would be assessed on their ability to design and plan a fair test, as well as their understanding of pressure.

The pupils were given some stimulus materials from the published scheme "Science in Process", which set them the problem of 'testing floor coverings to see how well they stand up to things pressing on them'. The pupils worked in groups of three or four which had been designated by the teacher. Each group was fairly mixed ability except for two which had some very 'bright' pupils in them.

As the pupils did the work, the teacher circulated amongst them asking to see their plan and discussing it with them. Several of the groups finished the task and went onto an activity about pressure, which explained the relationship between pressure and force. The teacher told pupils that she would be marking their work on this, but she also had time to talk to them about their ideas of pressure.

## SCENARIO 3

A year 3 class teacher reads the pupils a story, "Bimwili and the Zimwi". The story is about a girl who was captured and put into a drum. The pupils had a discussion about drums and examined a range of drums that were present in the room. Then they were asked to make a drum. Pupils presented their drum to the class and talked about the sounds it could make and anything they had found out about the drum. Some of the pupils worked in pairs while others worked individually. The teacher asked the pupils questions about the drums and the sounds they made, as they made them. During the presentation the other pupils could ask questions and the teacher made notes about the pupils' understandings of sound production and presentation skills.

## SCENARIO 4

A year 9 class werre studying their local school environment. The learning objectives of the activities that the pupils were undertaking included:

- to be able to identify that there are different organisms in leaf litter;
- to know that there are different numbers of each type of organism in leaf litter;
- to be able to identify the major groups of the organisms;
- to be able to recognise that there is a relationship between the different numbers of organisms;
- to be able to explain the pattern of numbers in relation to factors which affect variation in population size.

The teacher set the pupils a task of collecting and analysing leaf litter. The pupils had to identify the organisms using a key and draw a bar chart of the organisms. The pupils had to identify relationships between feeding and the numbers of the different types of organisms from the bar chart. The pupils also undertook an activity for determining camouflage. The pupils worked in mixed ability and gender groups of twos or threes as set by the teacher. The teacher talked to the pupils about their ideas of why they thought they got the different types of organisms in the leaf litter and made notes. The pupils had to show the teacher their final product of identification which the teacher had to agree with. The teacher marked the bar chart the pupils produced, and some questions on the relationships to population. However, for some pupils the teacher undertook a discussion with pupils about the variation in population.

# Pupil profiles

### DICON

Dicon is a boy born in the South-East of England, who is above average in ability. He is keen on science and likes doing 'experiments'. He is good at coming up with ideas and tends to lead a group in thinking through how to test out ideas. However he does not enjoy writing things down, and often fails to complete the written part of his work. His ability to talk to the whole class is good but he doesn't like using posters or O.H.P.s.

### FATMA

Fatma was born in a rural part of Turkey and has been in England for ten months. She likes school, has taken a while to settle down, but is now making good progress and seems to be learning quite quickly. She never learnt to write in Turkish but is now learning to read and write in English and Turkish. She has made a few friends but prefers to mix with other Turkish pupils in her class, or be with the ESL (English as a Second Language) support teacher.

### CLARE

Clare was born in London of Irish parents and speaks with an Irish accent. She loves school and mixes well with other pupils, though she can be quite shy with teachers. She writes extremely well but she does not like taking part in class presentations or discussion. Clare is of above average ability.

## JULIE

Julie was born in Britain but her parents originate from Jamaica. She attends the local Afro-Caribbean Saturday school and is extremely self confident. She speaks English with a local accent and also often talks in dialect. Her written skills are around average for her age, but she excels in discussion work – when she is often challenging and critical, and contributes many ideas. She is extremely popular but can tend to dominate quieter pupils.

## TARIQ

Tariq was born in Bangladesh, but came to Britain when he was a baby. He is highly motivated in school and produces highly imaginative written work in English. He speaks Sylheti at home and to his Bangladeshi friends in school. He does not, however, enjoy practical work and does not operate well in a group when practical work is being done, although he enjoys other discussion activities.

## DARREN

Darren was born in the North of England but moved from there to his present school in the Midlands two years ago. He has a wicked sense of humour and likes playing practical jokes which makes him alternately popular and unpopular with his class mates. During activities he either gets totally involved and produces excellent work or is disruptive. His reading and writing are average but he has to be pushed into doing any written work. His presentation skills are excellent and he often has the class 'in stitches'.

## ACTIVITIES 1 & 2                                                        TASK

You have been provided with a set of context cards. Each one describes a different situation which involves the grouping of pupils/students in a classroom.

**1** In turn, each group member reads out a card and, taking on the role described, gives a response as to what s/he would do in the situation described. The rest of the group then discuss and comment on the situation, and the response given. Spend no more than five minutes on each card, and ensure that each has been discussed.

**2** Select one of the cards which you feel is most interesting and/or challenging to you as a group. For the situation chosen, consider and discuss the question: "What are the implications in this situation for equality of opportunity and access for the pupil(s)/student(s) concerned?" Note the main conclusions of your discussion for reporting back to the full group.

## CONTEXT CARDS

**1** You are team teaching in an infant class. It is the turn of 'blue group' to use the construction kit. During the session, the two boys gradually take over and they dominate the task, so that only they are 'on-task'. One girl watches, while the other is left playing aimlessly with spare bricks. Your colleague is worried and doesn't know how to deal with the situation…What do you do?

**2** You are a class teacher. The class are involved in practical science investigations. A new pupil who speaks Panjabi, but little English, has joined the class. She seems to have difficulty in understanding the tasks when you explain them to her…How can you support her?

**3** You are a team leader. A collegue, worried that boys seem to be dominating practical science activities, has decided to introduce single sex groupings for practical work. She has also introduced a wider range of activities which she feels girls might be more interested in, and is giving groups a limited choice of these. You have your doubts about the approach…What do you do?

**4** You are a classroom teacher. Free-choice friendship-groups have been operating in the class for a long time, but you have noticed that this has led to boys and girls, and white and black pupils/students not working together. Several groups are losing motivation and are not producing very good written or practical outcomes. You would like to tackle this problem…How do you do it?

**5** You are a Year Head. For practical activities in a colleague's classroom, a number of Bangladeshi girls always seem to work together, speaking in Bengali. The teacher wants to split them up as he feels that they are not "mixing" and that he is never sure if they are 'on-task' (because he cannot understand what they are saying). The girls are unhappy and have complained. He asks for your advice…What do you say?

**6** You are a class teacher. In order to ensure that pupils work with others of similar ability, your year team decides upon work groups for science and maths based on ability (using relative performance in Teacher Assessments). In your classroom you begin to notice an increase in disruptive behaviour and a fall in the quality of work – particularly from pupils in the 'slower' groups. You would like to discuss this with your year team…How can you approach this?

**7** You are a team leader. You have a policy that there should be mixed groupings – both in terms of gender and ethnicity – for practical and collaborative work, and for assessment purposes. An Afro-Caribbean student in a colleague's class has complained to you that he is being 'shut-out' of his group on grounds of colour. He says he would like to be in an all-black group. The other Afro-Caribbean students in the class seem quite happy in their groups, and are not keen on the idea. The teacher claims there isn't a problem. How do you deal with the situation?

................................................................

**8**  You are a class teacher. A Vietnamese pupil who speaks English reasonably well is, you feel, underachieving. She hardly ever speaks in lessons and does not play an active role in group activities. She seems to have no friends in the class and, although you have put her in group with pupils you consider to be the most caring and capable, the situation has not improved. Lately you have heard some of the class making comments about her and you fear that these may become racist in nature. What can you do?

**9**  You are a year leader. Following an incident during break-time, tempers are running high. Your colleague reports to you that, on coming into the classroom and introducing a practical science investigation, one of the white girls was heard to say "I'm not working with any Pakis", and her comment was supported by several other members of the class. The girl has been sent to you and has acknowledged that she should not have made the comment, but cites a 'racial' fight in the playground as the reason. How do you deal with the situation, and what advice can you give to the class teacher regarding the group as a whole?

**10**  You are a member of the senior management team. A recent L.E.A. inspection report was very critical of what they saw as a disproportionately high number of black pupils in lower sets for Maths and Science. Staff who teach these subjects are annoyed, pointing out that 'setting' is school policy, is based purely on results in end of year assessments and that there is no 'bias'. They point out that there are a number of Asian boys in the top sets and claim that the criticism is unfair. How do you respond to the L.E.A. and to your staff?

Can we make a statement of principle which would guide us in the fair grouping of pupils/students to enable access and achievement for all?

# Notes on photos provided

**PHOTO 1**

Tigray Province, Ethiopia, January 1985. An inventor at the Tigre People's Liberation Front's technical institute with a new kind of water pump. In areas under the control of the T.P.L.F., workshops and training are run which focus on development projects such as electrification, water, etc. (*Mike Goldwater: Network*)

**PHOTO 2**

Pakistan, November 1986. Woman studying at the Afghan Women's Health Centre in Peshawar, North West frontier province, provided for Afghan refugees. (*Denis Doran: Network*)

**PHOTO 3**

Kaipos Indian during a demonstration and media event at Altamira in Amazonia, Brazil, February 1989. The Indians are protesting about the building of a dam which will flood their land. They are fighting to save their own land and the rainforest. (*Monique Cabrel: Format*)

**PHOTO 4**

Guarjila resettlement camp, El Salvador. Refugees who have returned from Honduras take part in a biology class. (*Jenny Matthews: Network*)

**PHOTO 5**

Spinning cotton on a machine being developed and tested at the Khadi Commission Centre in Ahmedebad, India. It is hand operated without the need for power, portable, and more efficient than the traditional 'charka'. Production of yarn is decentralised away from big mills. (*Sue Darlow: Format*)

**PHOTO 6**

Beijing, China, 1986. Traditional Chinese Medicine store. (*Laurie Sparham: Network*)

**PHOTO 7**

Nicaragua – fishing in the highly polluted Lake Managua. (*Jenny Matthews: Network*)

**PHOTO 8**

Girls picking traditional 'famine' foods in Narth Darfur, Sudan, December 1990. The green 'mokhed' berries must be dried, crushed and the seeds winnowed out of them. The seeds must then be soaked in water which is changed three times a day for a week. They are bitter and poisonous at first but after a week can be boiled and ground like millet. (*Network*)

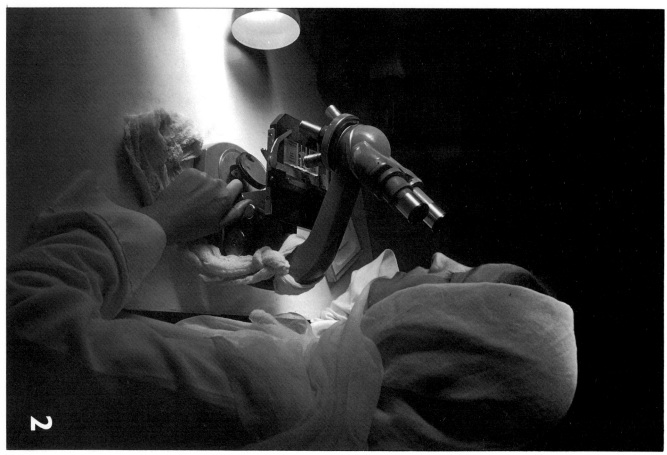

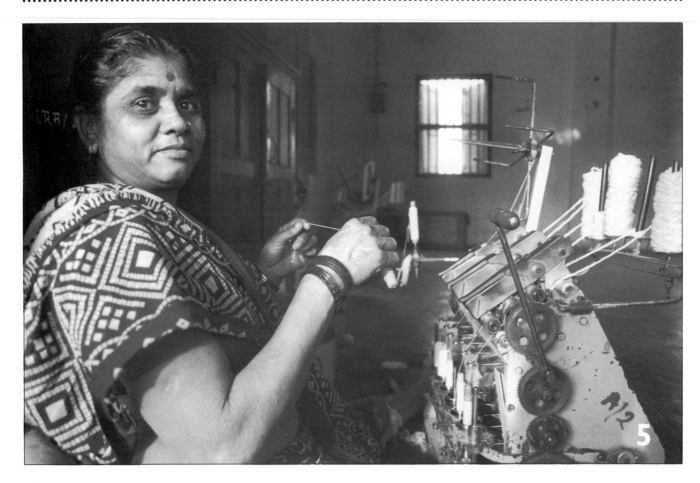

# Cropping template: photo 3

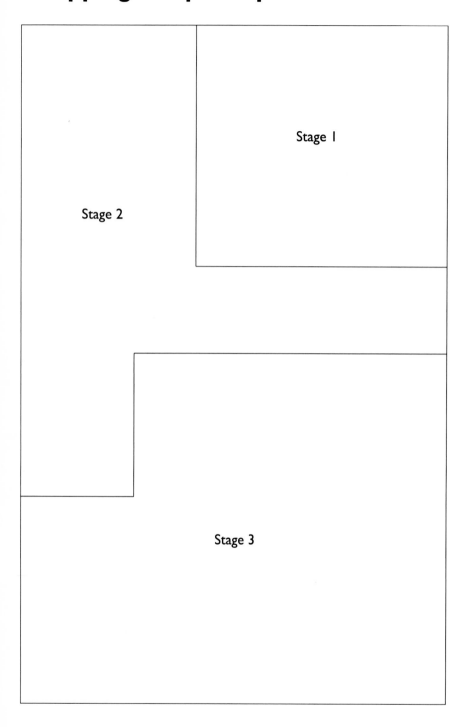

**Instructions**

Make two copies of template and cut the first to reveal Stage 1) and the second to reveal Stage 2).

Tape Stage 1) template over Stage 2) template and place over and tape to copy of photograph. Each group gets one set. Then proceed with exercise.

Note: If it is possible, enlarge copy of photo and template to A4 size before use.

# Cropping template: photo 5

Stage 1

Stage 2

Stage 3

**Instructions**

Make two copies of template and cut the first to reveal
Stage 1) and the second to reveal Stage 2).

Tape Stage 1) template over Stage 2) template and
place over and tape to copy of photograph. Each group
gets one set. Then proceed with exercise.

Note: If it is possible, enlarge copy of photo and
template to A4 size before use.

# CHOOSING A PHOTO

■ Look for the science in the photo.

■ Choose a photo that you:
  - like best;
  - find most interesting;
  - would like to find out more about.

■ Discuss these points with other colleagues.

## WHY USE PHOTOGRAPHS?

Photographs are images which:

- portray viewpoints of people and places;
- can be interpreted in different ways;
- can perpetuate stereotypes;
- can challenge assumptions and raise issues of equality and justice.

Using photographs in the classroom:

- can provide access to *all* children;
- does not assume literacy in English;
- involves collaborative working;
- can make children into 'critical observers';
- can encourage empathy and understanding;
- can build on children's experience and viewpoints;
- can support cross-curricular approaches.

# Why use photographs?

Media images – in the form of photographs – are often used to portray particular viewpoints and assumptions about people and places. However, like science itself, these images are often seen out of context and are interpreted in certain ways. Using photographs in a critical, challenging way with children and students can help them to challenge these viewpoints and assumptions and, hence, become 'critical observers' of the world around them. Because stereotypes are often perpetuated by 'images' – using photographs critically can be a positive tool for equality and justice.

On another level photographs, used as a stimulus for discussion in the classroom, are particularly accessible to *all* children and students. They do not assume literacy in English, they enable children to respond flexibly and on their own terms and, used sensitively, encourage empathy and understanding of others. Most activities using photographs are also collaborative and, therefore, promote access and language development for all children.

Photographs are also resources that teachers and children can produce themselves, and can provide an excellent way of building on, and discussing, the experiences and viewpoints of children and students in the classroom. Photography and photographs can be a stimulus for art, technology, media study and speaking and listening in English, historical and geographical studies and, not least, can support programmes of study in science at all key stages.

# Some ways of using photographs

## CROPPING

Using a series of template overlays, by cutting up or folding copies of a photo, 'cropping' can enable children to recognise that assumptions of an image may be stereotyped and that seeing a portion of an image can change meaning. An initial section of a photo is shown, and groups asked to discuss and write down what they think is happening in the photo: "Who is it?"; "What are people doing?"; "Where is it?" etc. At each stage more of the photo is revealed and the same questions asked. When the whole image is revealed, children/students are asked if they were surprised and how their view of the photo changed at each stage. An alternative is for groups to write captions for photos at each stage.

## FRAMING

Children are used to seeing photos within frames. Children are asked to frame an image in a photo they would like others to see or guess about. Each group can be given the same photo and frames to compare, or different photos for sharing and guessing. Discussion takes place around such questions as: "Why did you choose that image to frame?" and "What have you left out, and why?" Children can challenge their own preconceptions and prejudices about images and people. Another activity is for children to guess what was outside the frame when the picture was taken and to draw the details that they believe might have been omitted.

## CAPTIONS

When photographs are seen in magazines, newspapers and books, they often have captions which can change meaning. Pupils can be asked to caption a photo or set of photos. At its simplest, this will involve writing what the group thinks that the photo shows. Discussion can take place about why different captions emerged, and assumptions about ethnicity, gender roles, class, disability, etc. addressed. With older pupils, captions could be written for different publications, e.g. a school magazine, a national tabloid newspaper, a magazine concerned with development issues, a children's magazine or newspaper, a local newspaper, a book about science, a leaflet from Friends of the Earth, a community language newspaper/publication, etc., to show that purpose, viewpoint and audience also dictates meaning. Note that captions don't necessarily have to be in English.

## CHOOSING AND RANKING

Groups and/or individuals are asked to choose a favourite photo or photos based on criteria such as: "Which do you like best?"; "Which do find most interesting?"; "Which do you find most surprising?"; "Which illustrates our topic/viewpoint best?"; "Which could we use in our project/publication?"; "Which show science and/or scientists?" etc. The same range of questions can be used for ranking sets of photographs, with the most interesting/relevant, etc. at a top of a ladder, pyramid or diamond pattern. Discussion can focus on those ranked first and last, with groups able to challenge the choices and interpretations of others. This can enable exploration of notions such as "What is science?" and "Who are scientists?" – essential to the re-interpretation of science required for 'equality and justice' issues to be addressed.

## SEQUENCING AND MATCHING

Photos taken by children or teachers, or from photopacks, can be used for these activities which are essential to the development of language and for number work, as well as scientific processes. For matching use two identical sets of photos. Young children match pairs while being introduced to positive images and artefacts from different home and cultural backgrounds. Sequencing is a collaborative group or pair activity, captions, speech bubbles, writing and taping reports, stories, group presentations, etc. can be used as follow-up activities. One version to explore viewpoints is for pupils to produce a documentary or commentary on a set of photos. The same set can be given to each group, and each group given a role of someone in the community or involved with the issue being discussed. The groups write, record on tape, or present a documentary, and the different viewpoints are compared and discussed. This can be particularly useful in addressing different viewpoints on environmental, economic or development issues.

## QUESTIONING

Used to get children (and adults) to question their initial assumptions about an image, and to examine a photo in more depth than they might normally do. Groups are given a piece of paper on which is mounted the photograph. They are asked to write around the photograph as many questions as they can about what it shows. These are displayed around the room or presented in a plenary session. Pupils can be encouraged to consider whether any of the questions could be answered, and how the questions posed might affect their initial view of the image. The questions may also be useful as stimuli for more in-depth study and investigation.

## DRAMA STRUCTURES

A number of drama structures can be used in the classroom to raise awareness, encourage empathy and sharpen understanding of concepts and issues – including those of equality and justice. Many of the activities already listed are useful preliminary activities to these structures.

**Hot seating:** pupils are asked if there is anyone in the photo they would like to question/talk to/interview. A pupil (or teacher) takes the role and the rest of the group ask questions. Discussion, out of role, takes place around the questions and responses/viewpoints expressed.

**Freezing:** each group is given a photo and is asked to act out the events leading up to the moment in the photo, and ending up in a frozen statue of the image. These are presented to the group and then discussed.

**Statues:** Each group forms a sculpture or statue of their photo, trying to ensure that facial expressions, mannerisms, actions are realistically reproduced. Other groups can guess what the photo shows or what people are thinking or doing. The teacher can use thought-tapping by tapping a member of the statue group on the shoulder who then says what s/he (in role) is thinking at that moment.

## TAKING THEIR OWN

Photos taken by the pupils and/or teacher will have particular relevance to their own experience. Photos taken can include: records of class visits, activities, projects, etc., photo 'tours' of a local environment, self portraits and pictures of families, friends, homes, artefacts, each other, the school, etc. Most of the activities above can be carried out using sets of photos taken by the teacher and pupils. Photos can also be exchanged as part of links with another school in this country or abroad.

## RESOURCES

There are many photopacks on the market, but many excellent photo-images for classroom use can be found in newspapers and magazines. If you do use these check the copyright, and contact the publication direct for permission to take classroom copies. Some of the best photo resources for addressing equality issues have been produced by the Development Education Centre in Birmingham – and many of the activities above can be found in these packs. Particularly useful in compiling this handout have been *Get the Picture*, *Working Now*, *What is a Family?*, *Behind the Scenes* and *Hidden Messages*. Contact the D.E.C. at Selly Oak Colleges, Bristol Road, Birmingham, B29 6LE for information.

# The cola can curriculum 1

On this sheet is a picture of a cola can.  In your small group discuss what questions you could pose, or issues you could explore in the classroom to make the can the centre of a scheme of work which:

- includes practical investigations in science;
- addresses issues of equality and justice;
- uses global context(s).

Note down all your ideas for feeding back to the whole group.

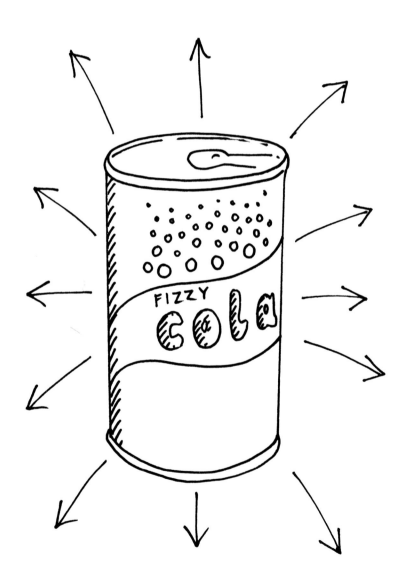

# The cola can curriculum 2

Below are a number of questions and issues which could be raised from the previous activity. In groups discuss and compare these ideas with your own and add any questions/comments if you wish.

Then discuss:

- what science could be done as part of a scheme of work based on this sheet;
- what you feel are the possible advantages and disadvantages for teachers and students of working in this way.

Note down your main points for reporting back to the whole group.

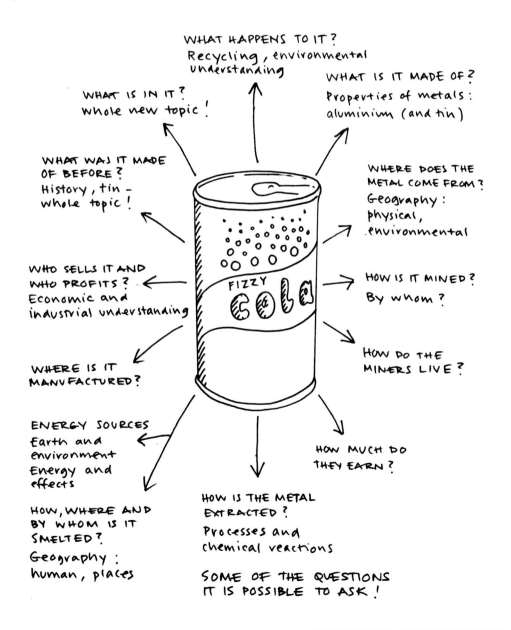

WHAT HAPPENS TO IT?
Recycling, environmental understanding

WHAT IS IN IT?
whole new topic!

WHAT IS IT MADE OF?
Properties of metals:
aluminium (and tin)

WHAT WAS IT MADE OF BEFORE?
History, tin – whole topic!

WHERE DOES THE METAL COME FROM?
Geography:
physical,
environmental

WHO SELLS IT AND WHO PROFITS?
Economic and industrial understanding

HOW IS IT MINED?
By whom?

WHERE IS IT MANUFACTURED?

HOW DO THE MINERS LIVE?

ENERGY SOURCES
Earth and environment
Energy and effects

HOW MUCH DO THEY EARN?

HOW, WHERE AND BY WHOM IS IT SMELTED?
Geography:
human, places

HOW IS THE METAL EXTRACTED?
Processes and chemical reactions

SOME OF THE QUESTIONS IT IS POSSIBLE TO ASK!

**ACTIVITY 1**                                                                    **TASK**

· · · · · · · · · · · · · · · · · · · · · · · · · · · · · · · · · · · · · · · · · · · · · · · · · · · · · · · · · · · · · · · · · · · ·

You have been provided with two systems diagrams.

First study the diagrams and discuss, in pairs, what you think they might be about and what they might show.

The look at the science in the systems and consider the following questions, making notes for sharing with another pair:

- What are the scientific principles in each system?
- What are the main differences between the systems?
- Who is 'doing' the science in each system?
- Can you put a name to each system and/or sum up the systems in a few words?
- Where do you think the systems operate?

Now share your perceptions with another pair and discuss what questions you might like answered about the diagrams.

· · · · · · · · · · · · · · · · · · · · · · · · · · · · · · · · · · · · · · · · · · · · · · · · · · · · · · · · · · · · · · · · · · · ·

# System I

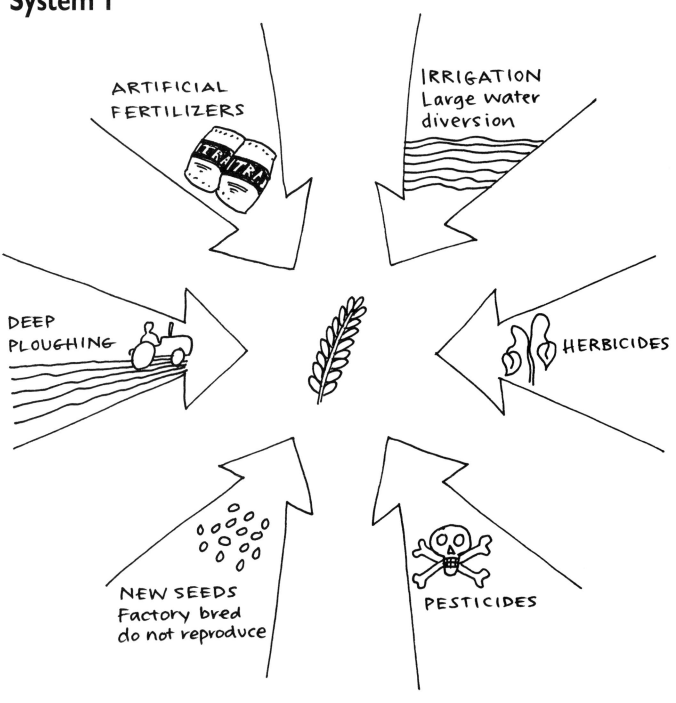

ARTIFICIAL FERTILIZERS

IRRIGATION Large water diversion

DEEP PLOUGHING

HERBICIDES

NEW SEEDS Factory bred do not reproduce

PESTICIDES

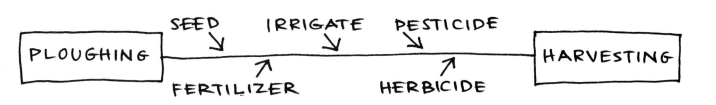

SEED

IRRIGATE

PESTICIDE

PLOUGHING

HARVESTING

FERTILIZER

HERBICIDE

# System 2

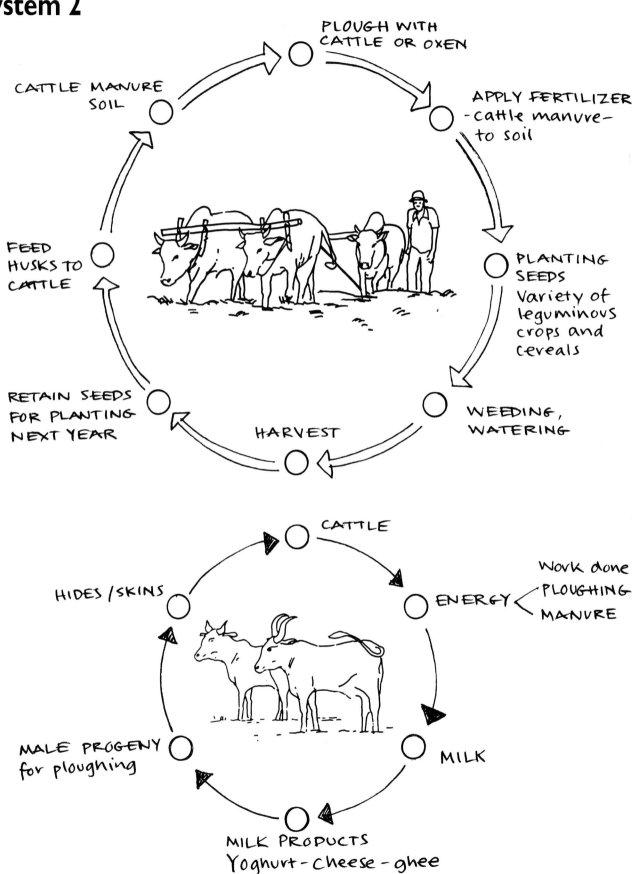

PLOUGH WITH CATTLE OR OXEN

CATTLE MANURE SOIL

APPLY FERTILIZER -cattle manure- to soil

FEED HUSKS TO CATTLE

PLANTING SEEDS Variety of leguminous crops and cereals

RETAIN SEEDS FOR PLANTING NEXT YEAR

HARVEST

WEEDING, WATERING

CATTLE

HIDES / SKINS

ENERGY

Work done PLOUGHING MANURE

MALE PROGENY for ploughing

MILK

MILK PRODUCTS Yoghurt - cheese - ghee

# SCIENCE SYSTEMS

- Reductionist **v** holistic?

- Non-sustainable **v** sustainable?

- Western knowledge **v** traditional knowledge?

- Employment and labour in each system?

- Imposed western 'solutions' to the problems of 'developing' countries?

- Profits **v** needs?

# The Green Revolution: A "Triumph" of Science?

High yield crops, fertilisers, pesticides – with the Green Revolution, science promised to put an end to world hunger.

## "Super seeds"

The first task given to the scientists producing the new "super seeds" was to breed out their self-reproducing character and genetic diversity. The resultant hybrid "miracle" seeds are a commercial miracle – farmers have to buy new supplies of them every year! These new varieties of seeds are called HYV or high-yielding variety – but this is true only in response to heavy inputs of irrigation and chemical fertilisers. They also have a vulnerability to pests and disease.

The Green Revolution was born in Mexico in the early 1940's. It was exported to the rest of the world as a guarantee that "famine and hunger need never again blight the peoples of the world". A new government in Mexico in the 1930's saw "industrial greatness" as the new goal and agrarian reforms, rural health and education programmes took a back seat. The U.S. was hungry for cheap Mexican produced food and goods to support the war effort. In 1943 the Mexican government welcomed the Rockefeller Foundation to the country and together they launched the "green revolution".

## Emilio's story

" I can remember my parents talking about things getting better – the yields of corn and beans had improved with Government help" says Emilio, a poor Mexican farmer. But with the coming of the green Revolution things rapidly deteriorated. "All of a sudden, it was science this and science that. Government officials told us they had developed new seeds and fertilizers and pesticides which would increase growth, kill off insects and stop plant diseases. But when we asked for help in obtaining them, we were told that they were not suitable for the type of crops we wanted to produce. They were for irrigated land. They said we would have to change our farming methods. When we asked how we could do this they told us it would cost a lot of money and that credit was only available to what they called 'viable enterprises'. They told us to carry on producing beans and corn as best we could".

Unable to purchase the "inputs" for their plot, more and more effort went into producing less and less. Eventually these farmers were forced to rent their land to a Mexico City market-gardening company. Now the land is producing a rich crop of tomatoes for sale in California and Texas. The green revolution was not for the people of Mexico, they are enduring more and more hardship. As in Africa and South America the green revolution has been aimed at producing cash crops for sale overseas.

## Women's work

Women everywhere are farming to grow what food they can to feed the family. They fetch water and wood and look after the children alone, while more and more men leave the rural areas for work in the factories, or wherever they can find it. It is the women's labour that underpins production of cash crops. As more land is diverted to cash crops and is impoverished through the ecological impact of green revolution technologies, the "value" of women's work and status falls, while their work in producing food for survival increases. By splitting the agricultural economy into a cash-mediated male sector and a subsistence, food producing female sector, the work burden and marginalisation of women is simultaneously increased.

The development of high yielding seeds boosted the production of wheat and rice, two of the world's major food crops. These seeds worked wonders on farms with good soil, plentiful water and enough capital or credit for the necessary fertilizers and insecticides. That brought immense benefits to medium and large farmers in areas already favoured by nature. But they did little to help small farmers growing staples like beans, cassava, yam millet, sorghum and maize.

## "Dwarf cereals" and "Super cattle"

Traditional cereals, characterised by tall, thin straw, could not support the new heavy seeds, so dwarf varieties were bred. In India the new plants meant that women lost the crop wastes which are fed to cattle. These traditional cattle produce food, in the form of milk, in excess of the edible food consumed – in contrast to the cows introduced from the West which eat six times as much edible food as is obtained from them! The male progeny of the traditional cattle provide more than two-thirds of the power requirements of Indian villages, the equivalent of a thousand million US dollars in petrol each year. The cattle also provide 700 million tonnes of recoverable manure, half of which is used as fuel, the other half as fertiliser. 150 million dollars is earned annually from the export of hides, skins etc. The reductionist scientists saw only the seeds and pronounced them low-yielding, they did not see the complexity of agriculture; they saw only cows with low milk yields and decided that the answer was to introduce high yielding cows, ignoring all their other uses.

The new crops needed intensive irrigation, they diverted the rivers or sunk tube-wells, they ignored the needs of villages for water and they ignored the invisible job done by the underground river in replenishing the ground water supplies. Governments ploughed vast sums of money into irrigation projects, turning areas of land in northern Mexico into open-air factories producing grain and animal foodstuffs for the U.S. The peasants in Mexico were forced to sell up because of the pressure put on them by soaring land prices. The mechanisation of agriculture also meant fewer jobs in the countryside.

## Reductionist science

The new crops need fertilisers and pesticides. Scientist ignored the natural fertiliser provided by the cows and green manure grown by the women and they ignored the natural pest protection from intercropping. At each stage the reductionist view has ignored the complexity of the agriculture which existed already.

"With the centralised production and transfer of HYV seeds has come the transfer of diseases. Gone is the resistance built on diversity; in its place comes vulnerability. Gone is nature as a source for seeds; in its place comes agri-business and seed corporations. Gone is the local knowledge of millions of tribals and peasants; in its place comes one centralised research institute with largely male, largely white "experts" who prescribe green revolution rice agriculture to farmers...The result has been a total undermining of the ecology and economics of rice farming in particular and agriculture in general."

*Vandana Shiva*

The green revolution has assumed that the nutrient loss in the soil can be made up by use of non-renewable inputs. Western reductionist thinking is using a model which is non-sustainable. Today, all over India, crop failures are being reported. At the same time soil toxicity is spreading. The soil, depleted of organic matter and nutrient, has introduced the nitrate pollution of water systems through chemical fertilizers, and the pesticide pollution of entire ecosystems. These are ecological imbalances created by the nutrient demands of high-yielding varieties.

## Blame the victim

As scientists flock to the "Third World" in search of solutions to dying soils they often blame the victims. But the true cause is western science which, with its highly energy-intensive, chemical intensive, water intensive and capital intensive agricultural techniques, has created deserts out of fertile soils in less than two decades. It has spread rapidly across the "Third World" in the form of agricultural development, accelerated by the green revolution and financed by international development and aid agencies.

Science applied to agriculture has moved from seeing farming as a process of nurturing the earth to maintain her capacity to provide food, to farming as a process of generating profits. Ecological destruction is one inevitable result of this commercialisation. Peasant farmers throughout the "Third World" have recognised that too much cultivation and deep ploughing would destroy the balance of soil fertility and soil is being lost through the use of farming methods which ignore these truths. Throughout the world today, tractors, seen as the pinnacle of farming technology, are employed, alongside the fertilizers and pesticides, as part of the "scientific" approach to farming. Tropical soils are thin and fragile, the green revolution ignored this and, as a consequence, soil is literally blowing away rendering vast areas of land barren. Again the peasant farmers suffer while the green revolution moves on.

**Alyson Jenkins**

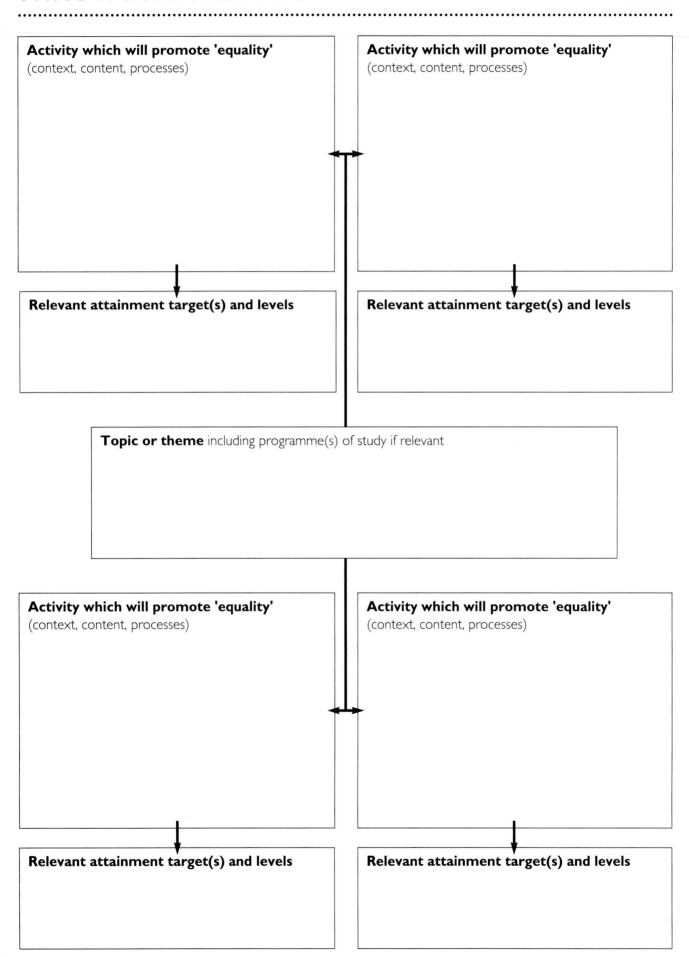

**Activity which will promote 'equality'**
(context, content, processes)

**Activity which will promote 'equality'**
(context, content, processes)

**Relevant attainment target(s) and levels**

**Relevant attainment target(s) and levels**

**Topic or theme** including programme(s) of study if relevant

**Activity which will promote 'equality'**
(context, content, processes)

**Activity which will promote 'equality'**
(context, content, processes)

**Relevant attainment target(s) and levels**

**Relevant attainment target(s) and levels**

........................................................................

**Activity which will promote 'equality'**
(context, content, processes)

TELLING THE STORY
- Context is 'global', positive images
- Listening to story on tape in home language supports developing bilinguals, values home experience
- Re-telling using magnet board: language development, collaborative work

**Activity which will promote 'equality'**
(context, content, processes)

'MAKING' A DRUM
- Investigate best materials to use, builds on each child's experience
- Mixed ability groups investigate one variable: provides access for all
- Vote on 'best' material: promotes democracy/equality
- Groups formed to enable first language work: values language, draws on experience

**Relevant attainment target(s) and levels**

English ATs at KSI

**Relevant attainment target(s) and levels**

Science: ATI levels 1a, 2a, 2b, 2c, 3a, 3b, 3d
AT4 levels 1b, 3b
AT3 levels 1a, 2b, 3b

**Topic or theme** including programme(s) of study if relevant

BIMWILI AND THE ZIMWI : Story based theme

P of S   1 "Making and experiencing sounds, etc... using
(Science)   familiar objects and musical instruments from
a variety of cultures..."
2 "Collect and find similarities and differences
in a variety of everyday materials"

**Activity which will promote 'equality'**
(context, content, processes)

DRAWING POSTERS,
COMMUNICATING FINDINGS

**Activity which will promote 'equality'**
(context, content, processes)

WHAT HAVE WE FOUND OUT?
BRAINSTORMING AND
EVALUATION

**Relevant attainment target(s) and levels**

**Relevant attainment target(s) and levels**

**Activity which will promote 'equality'**
(context, content, processes)

PRACTICAL INVESTIGATIONS
ON ENERGY TRANSFERS

**Activity which will promote 'equality'**
(context, content, processes)

ANALYSIS OF DATA IN
GLOBAL CONTEXT

**Relevant attainment target(s) and levels**

Various statements and levels
related to AT1 and AT4

**Relevant attainment target(s) and levels**

Various statements and levels
related to AT1 and AT4

**Topic or theme** including programme(s) of study if relevant
WORLD ENERGY RESOURCES : Science topic involving
Programme of study
re: "energy transfers in a variety of personal and
practical contexts." and "consider the longer term
implications of the worldwide patterns of
distribution and use of energy resources"

**Activity which will promote 'equality'**
(context, content, processes)
PROJECTS ON 'ALTERNATIVES'
Case studies made by groups on
energy projects "in global context"
● Collaborative activity enhances
access
● contexts – photovoltaics in Pakistan
        – wave power in Mauritius
        – bioenergy in Brazil
positively value 'Third World' science
● Issues  – local needs versus
imposed solutions addresses 'colonialism'
'racism' in energy and industry

**Activity which will promote 'equality'**
(context, content, processes)

**Relevant attainment target(s) and levels**
AT4 levels 4c, 5d, 5e, 6c, 6d
        7d, 7e, 9c

**Relevant attainment target(s) and levels**

## STAGE 2: ACTIVITY 3                                    TASK

You have started to make connections between National Curriculum content and processes and principles of equality and justice.

For the topic chosen for the previous activity, in pairs consider how your existing schemes of work (already in place for the topic chosen), could be modified in the light of equality and justice issues.

Use the principles below to help you and note any particular modifications which you make and which might be interesting to share with others in the group.

## PRINCIPLES OF EQUALITY AND JUSTICE IN THE SCIENCE CURRICULUM

The science curriculum should emphasise:

- that science is a cultural activity practiced in particular social, political and economic contexts;
- that science is not neutral or value free – scientists are influenced by the environment in which they work;
- the interplay of science, technology and society;
- the false genetic basis by which racism is supported.

The teaching and learning of science should:

- promote a study of the nature of science;
- encourage the teaching of process skills and attitudes;
- help pupils question the reasons underlying inequalities between peoples and nations, and to relate such issues to those of interdependence;
- question and challenge racist attitudes and assumptions;
- provide positive images and avoid stereotypes of people places and times;
- show science as a worldwide activity;
- build on learners' cultural background and experiences;
- value and develop learners' linguistic repertoire;
- provide specific support for the language development of bilingual learners.

Opportunities to demonstrate achievement should ensure:

- consistency between the language of teaching and learning,, and the language of assessment;
- that contexts for assessment are no less broad than those of the curriculum;
- that assessment forms an integral part of, and enhances, teaching and learning;
- the use of appropriate assessment strategies to ensure that all pupils can show what they 'know, understand and can do';
- that pupils' ability to communicate their understanding is not limited by their language 'register'.

# Policy development and review: introduction

This section provides a systematic process-based exploration of the nature of policy development, implementation and review. It is intended to:

- enable groups of teachers to develop and implement policies which:
  - build on the awareness gained in previous workshops in this manual;
  - are relevant to their particular school, department or institution;
- offer the option of working with case study materials which:
  - illustrate various approaches in different institutions. OR
  - use the processes within a school or department to develop and implement actual policy.

It is based on the viewpoint that policy formation must be process-based and dynamic, and that the implementation of policy (particularly when dealing with issues of equality and anti-racism) needs to be thoroughly planned and monitored. It also assumes that all the issues raised and addressed in this manual related to science education, need to considered within a whole-school policy approach to equality and anti-racism. The section is supported by the paper "Developing policy for equality" which discusses these issues further and can be used as a handout, or as a basis for O.H.P. slides, etc., in introductory/plenary sessions.

Because the workshops, taken together, form a coherent process model for policy development and implementation, it is recommended that they are worked through sequentially in the order below. Facilitators should read all the procedures and notes thoroughly before use and decide on appropriate scenarios and contexts for the particular group of teachers worked with. If the group is developing an actual policy, then the workshops can be adapted to fit in with the school's or department's own planning models or patterns of meetings. Note that the processes and models in the final workshop "Individual/group action planning" may also be useful in supporting other workshops, particularly in the "Curriculum issues" section of this manual.

As the policy workshops are sequential, it is suggested that evaluation is carried out at the end of the whole section.

## THE WORKSHOPS

**1 Who is policy for?** aims to raise awareness of the range of groups interested in school policy and practice, and what their expectations of the school science policy might be, through small group and plenary brainstorm and discussion activities.

**2 What is in a policy?** aims to raise awareness of how policy can relate to, and respond to, particular contexts and stimuli whilst still being broad and developmental, using a group simulation exercise and plenary discussions.

**3 How is policy produced?** aims to enable a group to decide on the mechanism by which they can produce the policy they need and to provide support to the task of generating elements of policy through the generation of policy statements in small groups and plenary discussions.

**4 How do we put policy into practice?** aims to enable teachers to devise strategies for putting policy into practice, and to develop criteria by which the success of these strategies can be evaluated, using structured pro-formas to generate issues and indicators.

**5 Individual/group action planning** aims to provide teachers with the opportunity, as individuals or in groups, to reflect on the issues raised with relation to policy and practice in 'race equality and science teaching' and to plan manageable action for their school, college and/or team, using planning sheet activities.

# Who is policy for?

## PURPOSE

To raise awareness of the range of groups interested in school policy and practice and what their expectations of the school science policy might be.

## RESOURCES

Task sheets, pages 145–147.
Pens, paper, flipchart.

**Time: 60 minutes**

## PROCEDURE

Facilitator should introduce the session by stating the purpose and expected duration, and by providing some ideas of activities involved.

## ACTIVITIES

**1** In whole group generate a list of all people who may have an interest in, or be affected by, a school's science and equal opportunities policy. Facilitator records these on flipchart **5 minutes**

**2** Each groups of five or six is provided with task sheets. From the list they are to enter onto the pro-forma the six groups they think it would be most important to consult when framing a policy. **10 minutes**

**3** Each group divides into pairs. Each pair is allocated/chooses two groups from the six and generates a list of reasons how and why their group are interested in, or affected by, the school's policy. The pair then prioritise these reasons and enter four of these onto the second task sheet. Each person takes on a group and will report the reasons back to the larger group. **20 minutes**

**4** Each person reports back. A group 'scribe' enters the reasons on the grid provided, noting any similarities and differences. Each group chooses one group of *similar reasons* and one specific *different reason* to report back to the main group. **15 minutes**

**5** Groups report back and facilitator leads discussion around the questions "Are the similarities good points on which we can build action?", "Are the differences likely to be constructive or potential sources of conflict in policy formation?" **10 minutes**

## EVALUATION

As the evaluations are sequential, the facilitator is advised to do one evaluation at the end of the whole section, as part of the "Personal and group action plans" workshop.

## NOTES FOR FACILITATORS

*This introductory workshop on policy development and review is aimed at broadening the context in which the issues of 'race, equality and science teaching' is considered. It suggests that there are groups of people in the school and community who have an interest in, and will be affected by, school policy, and who may have different viewpoints and expectations of such policies.*

*In Activity 1 the facilitator should ask for a list of people who might be interested – these could include governors, parents, local community groups, students, non-teaching staff, etc. In choosing six interest groups to focus on, each group of five or six is prioritising and effectively establishing ownership of these interest groups.*

*In the subsequent group and pair activities, ownership is established further, and discussions will focus on the reasons and motives which each group might have in holding certain views or having an interest in the school.*

*Participants should be urged to discuss this in some depth, and to deal with positive and negative reasons. Also ensure that the participants are clear, throughout the workshop, that we are dealing with policy in relation to equality, and anti-racist issues in particular.*

*In the final summing up the facilitator should elicit ideas about what common interests and possible conflicts there might be for different interest groups when considering these issues. Are the needs/viewpoints of some groups more important/influential than others? What are the pointers for action which are implied by the results of this exercise?*

# What is in a policy?

## PURPOSE
To raise awareness of how policy can relate to, and respond to, particular contexts and stimuli whilst still being broad and developmental.

## RESOURCES
Scenario sheets, pages 148–153; handout, pages 154–155.
Paper, pens, flipchart, blank O.H.P. acetates, O.H.P.

**Time: 85 minutes**

## PROCEDURE
Facilitator should introduce the session by stating the purpose and expected duration, and by providing some ideas of activities involved.

Small groups of five to eight are given a task sheet and the guidance notes, "Managing a role play or simulation".

Scenario: Staff meeting(s) to discuss areas of policy for science and equal opportunities.

## TASK
To generate a list of ideas and proposals to be covered by the policy.

## ACTIVITIES
**1** Groups are asked to simulate a staff meeting – either whole staff, mixed staff, working group or department meeting – which is meeting for the first time, as specified on the workshop sheet. Their task is to consider what areas/issues a policy on science and equal opportunities would address. Groups can decide to employ a variety of strategies, but should generate a comprehensive but manageable list of issues to include and prepare a presentation for the plenary session.

**50 minutes**

**2** Each group gives presentation/feedback to whole group, and answers questions regarding points of clarification (not opinion at this stage). **20 minutes**

**3** Facilitator leads discussion to identify similarities, differences and any ommissions, and to discuss the implications of these for the development of policy.

**15 minutes**

### EVALUATION
As the evaluations are sequential, the facilitator is advised to do one evaluation at the end of the whole section, as part of the "Personal and group action plans" workshop.

## NOTES FOR FACILITATORS
*By placing the task of policy formation into a variety of real institutional contexts, participants can begin to understand the nature of policy formation as broad and developmental, yet specific to particular circumstances. The range of contexts provided are to deal with a range of 'combinations, e.g. a secondary science department writing a policy for equality and justice; a whole school policy for science in a multi-ethnic primary school, etc. Groups of five to eight should each take on one of these contexts, not necessarily one which they would all relate to directly in their own current experience; the facilitator may wish to construct mixed groups if this is being done with participants from different schools and phases.*

*In Activity 1, the simulation itself, groups should feel free to tackle the task using any approaches they feel appropriate as long as they stay within the context provided. The "Managing a role play or simulation" handout is recommended for reference. The presentation can be any form but will most obviously be a verbal report back accompanied by O.H.P. or flipchart aids. Blank O.H.P. slides, paper etc. should be made available. Timing should be judged by the facilitator who may wish to give more time for the simulation than the 50 minutes suggested.*

*In the report back and discussion in Activities 2 and 3, several points are important. First, during the feedback presentations there should be no discussion/criticism or comment by other members of the group. After the presentation, participants can ask questions relating to factual clarification, but not of opinion. In the discussion following, the facilitator should ask participants to look for similarities, differences and ommissions in order to build up some common principles for policy development and to identify those which might be specific to phase, type of school, etc. The purpose of the discussion should be to share ideas and perspectives between groups, to consider whether, and to what extent, a policy should be narrow and context-specific or all embracing. The facilitator should, at this stage, feed in any issues which have not been dealt with by the groups.*

# How is policy produced?

## PURPOSE
- to enable a group to decide on the mechanism by which they can produce the policy they need;
- to provide support to the task of generating elements of policy.

(N.B. this workshop can be used to guide actual practice, or as a simulation exercise. Options for this are provided below and further guidance is provided in the notes for facilitators).

## RESOURCES
Task sheet, page 156; policy cue cards, pages 157–159. Paper, pens, flipchart.

**Time: 120 minutes**

## PROCEDURE
Facilitator should introduce the session by stating the purpose and expected duration, and by providing some ideas of activities involved.

Scenario (for use in simulation): A school or department preparing a policy statement addressing science and equality issues (one scenario to be selected from those provided).

## ACTIVITIES
### Stage 1
Preparing for policy development.

## TASK
To consider what needs to be done to prepare for writing a policy.

**1** Facilitator introduces the scenario and tells participants "You have been assigned an issue to consider. Eventually you will prepare the statement on this issue to be included in a draft policy". **5 minutes**

**2** Groups of two or three are assigned an issue on an issue card (or from issues generated in a previous workshop), and carry out tasks on sheet 1, including who to consult, what information is needed. **30 minutes**

**3** In plenary session, small groups report back on people to consult and information they wish to seek. The facilitator collates two central lists of people to consult and information to seek and displays this for use in Stage 2. Group to discuss practical strategies such as who will do what and when; how and when they will feedback findings to the whole group, etc; **25 minutes**

## NOTES FOR FACILITATORS
*This workshop is intended to follow on from the previous two Policy workshops "Who is policy for?" and "What is in a policy?", and to provide a model for writing policy statements which delegates reponsibility for writing them on specific issues to small groups and collating these into a coherent policy statement on science and equality. The workshop is, therefore, suitable to be used in the actual production of a policy statement in a school or department, or as an INSET exercise working in simulation on one of the scenarios provided for the previous workshop; the facilitator should select the most appropriate for a particlar group. The process will be the same for either approach, except in Activity 4, where option activities are suggested.*

*If the workshop is being carried out as a way of producing an actual policy, then the following points need to be considered. In Activity 2 it is assumed that the issues/areas which the policy should cover will have already been generated in previous discussions (in an exercise similar to the previous "What is in a Policy?" workshop). Other than this, Activities 2 and 3 can run as described in the Procedure set out. Clearly, Activity 3 will involve setting an action plan and timetable including who is to consult whom, find out what and when/how feedback is to take place. A clear timetable, culminating in dates for writing and collating the policy statements should be set. In Activity 4, the tasks of consulting, finding out and writing statements will be spread over a number of weeks and may involve a number of small/group meetings and other research and consultative activities/visits/discussions. Activity 5 will be the final whole group meeting at which the statements are collated and the overall policy produced.*

*If the workshop is being carried out as an INSET simulation exercise, the following points need to be considered. It is important that the facilitator sets a scenario in which the whole group is to work. Suggested scenarios are provided, but other appropriate examples may be developed by the*

. . . . . . . . . . . . . . . . . . . . . . . . . . . . . . . . . . . . . . . . . . . . . . . . . . . . . . . . . . . . . . . . . . . . . . . . . . . . . . . . . .

### Stage 2
Writing policy statements

### TASK
To write and collate policy statements into an overall written policy on science and equality.

**4** (Simulation option) **a** Small groups given task sheet 2 and to imagine that they have made their enquiries and consultations; they discuss/note the kind of information and opinions that these might have elicited; **b** groups to write the statement on their issue/statement which could be included in the whole group's policy. **30 minutes**

(Writing actual policy option) Whole group need to decide action, set tasks for small groups and agree a timetable for consultation/information gathering and writing of statements. These tasks to be carried out and reported to whole group in meeting such as in 5 below.

**5** In plenary group, the individual statements are displayed and /or collated on flipchart/O.H.P. Facilitator invites group to discuss and revise individual statements looking at areas of overlap, re-organisation, ommission, balance, etc. in order to produce a coherent policy statement. **30 minutes**

---

### EVALUATION
As the evaluations are sequential, the facilitator is advised to do one evaluation at the end of the whole section, as part of the "Personal and group action plans" workshop.

---

*facilitator; this will depend on the participants involved and the nature/phase of the schools/institutions they are working in. If a cross-phase group is being trained then it may be appropriate to use the Middle School scenario and to stress that it is the processes of policy development which are important and these should be applied to participants' own school contexts. In Activity 2, issues/areas to be allocated may be those previously generated in the "What is in a policy?" workshop OR on the "Issues cards" provided. Issues are drawn from the sections of the discussion document in Appendix 1. In Activity 3, after the collation exercise, the discussion on "practical strategies such as who will do what and when; how and when they will feedback findings to the whole group", will deal with the implications of these questions and participants should be asked to draw on, and share, their own experiences in this discussion.*

*In Activity 4, small groups are asked to imagine that they have completed the consultation and research phase (within the scenario provided) and to consider the type of responses that may have resulted. This enables participants to consider further the views and perspectives of other interest groups (as raised in the Workshop "Who is a policy for?") and to best-guess the nature of information sought. Based on this imaginary information a draft statement on this issue should be produced.*

*In Activity 5, the facilitator should lead the discussion so that a coherent overall statement can be worked towards. It is not necessary, in the simulation option, that this final statement is actually produced (although it may be useful to do this and provide it as a handout) but certain issues need to be considered and the statements discussed and revised so that:*
*   *- overlap, clusters and reorganisation are discussed to produce a coherent statement;*
*   *- ommissions, imbalances and wording are identified which might detract from the quality and message of the final document.*

*The language used in the statements should be carefully considered; Appendix 2 may be useful in supporting this.*

# How do we put policy into practice?

## PURPOSE

To enable the teacher to devise strategies for putting policy into practice, and to develop criteria by which the success of these strategies can be evaluated.

## RESOURCES

Task sheet, page 160; guidance sheets, pages 161–163; blank pro-forma task sheets, pages164–165. Paper, pens, flipchart, O.H.P.

**Time: 90 minutes**

## PROCEDURE

Facilitator should introduce the session by stating the purpose and expected duration, and by providing some ideas of activities involved.

## NOTES FOR FACILITATORS

*This workshop is designed to take participants through a systematic process, beginning with a list of issues and ending up with quite specific criteria or 'indicators' by which they will be able to judge success. It is essential that careful monitoring and evaluation takes place so that equality promised in policy statements is actually received as entitlement by pupils/students and others in the school community. The workshop can be carried out in an INSET session, providing teachers with a model for policy implementation and monitoring, or in a school or college implementing an actual policy. Whichever way it is used we assume that schools and colleges would wish to ensure that developments in equality issues are seen as an integral part of their overall development plan, and that processes of review, prioritisation, consultation, etc. will already have taken place - possibly through using processes such as those in the "Initial reflections" and "Policy development and review" sections.*

*The facilitator will need to explain the activities in the workshop, and guidance sheets are provided showing the staged process of filling in the task sheets, using an example issue. The diagrams in these guidance sheets can also be used as O.H.P. originals to demonstrate how the workshop works.*

## ACTIVITIES

**1** Groups of three to five take on ownership of an issue, each of which is an identified aspect of a policy in 'race equality and science education"'. (From lists in previous workshops, or generated in an initial brainstorm.) The group is asked to discuss the question, "Can the issue be broken down into more specific areas for action?" A number of these are generated and then prioritised to three or four areas for action. These are then recorded on the first task sheet.

**20 minutes**

*In Activity 1, it is assumed that a list of issues has already been generated and worked with previously (see previous workshops in this section). If this is not the case, then time will be needed to generate such a list through a question such as "If you are considering a policy addressing race equality and science teaching in your school/college, what areas or issues would such a policy need to address?" An alternative is to use the key issues cue cards from the "How is policy produced" Workshop.*

**2** For one area of action recorded above, the group is asked to brainstorm a list of practical strategies which might be effective in addressing it in schools/colleges. These are then prioritised and no more than three strategies selected and entered on the flow chart on the second task sheet. **20 minutes**

*In Activity 2, when groups are asked to generate and prioritise strategies, three is considered the maximum number to be manageable, but groups should not feel they have to produce three; one or two good strategies may suffice.*

**3**   For the strategies identified, the group then discuss the question "How can we judge whether the strategy has worked or is working? What are the criteria or indicators of success?" These are then entered on the final column of the flow chart on the second task sheet.

**30 minutes**

(The groups may then wish to repeat Activities 2 and 3 for the other areas of action identified in 1.)

**4**   Each group reports back to a plenary on one of their areas of action mapped. Facilitator leads a discussion on the nature of the strategies and criteria used. Sheets can be collected in, collated and recirculated by facilitator.

**20 minutes**

---

**EVALUATION**

As the evaluations are sequential, the facilitator is advised to do one evaluation at the end of the whole section, as part of the "Personal and group action plans" workshop.

---

*In Activity 3 when criteria and/or indicators are being discussed, groups should note that some criteria/indicators may be the same or similar for more than one strategy. Similarly, strategies may have several criteria or indicators.*

*In an INSET session it may be useful to simply take one area for action of the three/four identified through to the indicators stage, as the process will have been illustrated and made clear. In a school or college implementing an actual policy this will not be the case and the timescales involved in the exercise will vary.*

*One further activity which might be useful for groups is to analyse their indicators as 'quantitative' (i.e. those that can be statistically measured and monitored) and 'qualitative' (which are not measured in numerical terms but may be based on comments, documents, observations, etc.) Similar analysis can distinguish those indicators specific to science and race equality issues, from those which are more general.*

*Follow up will again depend on how the workshop is used. In an INSET session a useful exercise following the report back and plenary session is for the facilitator to collect in all the sheets, to collate these and send a complete copy of all the groups' responses back to participants. A wide range of strategies, criteria and indicators will then be available for collegues to consider in their own schools/colleges. If the process is in implementing an actual policy, the team leader or senior management will need to ensure that the responses are collated in an accessible form for all staff; that responsibility of staff for implementation and monitoring of the strategies is clear, and that more specific timescales and targets are set based on the strategies and indicators.*

# Personal and group action plans

## PURPOSE

To provide teachers with the opportunity, as individuals or in groups, to reflect on the issues raised in relation to policy and practice in 'race equality and science teaching' and to plan manageable action for their school, college and/or team.

## RESOURCES

Action planning sheet, page 166; task/handout sheet, page 167.
Paper, pens, flipchart, O.H.P.

**Time: 60 minutes**

## PROCEDURE

Facilitator should introduce the session by stating the purpose and expected duration, and by providing some ideas of activities involved.

## ACTIVITIES

**1** In groups of two, three or four, participants discuss the question "Thinking back over the whole course of workshops in 'race equality and science teaching', what issues raised, or information provided, have been most useful, stimulating or require the most urgent action in our school(s)/college(s)?" This to be recorded in whatever form they wish on a large sheet of paper.
**20 minutes**

**2** Groups report back on their 'posters' to the whole group and the facilitator makes brief notes on flipchart or O.H.P.
**15 minutes**

**3** Individuals (or groups/teams) fill in the Action planning sheet, choosing issues they feel most important to address under the headings, "Where do I/we start?"; "What are my/our longer term goals?"; "How will I/we know when we are successful?" and "Any other comments".
**25 minutes**

## NOTES FOR FACILITATORS

*Personal and group action plans act both as a simple tool for reviewing and planning in the school and team environment, and as an evaluative activity for the course of workshops in this manual. The questions at the head of the action planning sheet can form the basis of group discussion or of individual reflection and the exercise is designed to be used flexibly. Such an approach may, for example, be useful in considering more specific issues dealt with in other workshops and sections in this manual.*

*Returning to the aide-memoire approach used in the "Initial reflections" section may also assist in the process of developing action plans – and for this purpose a short checklist is provided which can form the basis of reflection or discussion. An alternative is for groups to return to their original responses in the "Initial Reflections" section and review these in the light of the course of INSET the participants have been through.*

*Reference to the paper "Developing policy for equality" may also help in this process and, in particular, the "Cycle of institutional change and development" diagram. Facilitators will note that there is some overlap with the other workshops in this section, especially the "How do we put policy into practice?" workshop. Facilitators may wish to use a variation on these action planning processes as a preliminary/alternative to that workshop, although the indicators produced will not be as precise or systematic in nature.*

### EVALUATION

This workshop is, in itself, a kind of evaluation of the whole course - but the action plan sheets will be kept by the participants. Additional evaluation should be provided to to review the effectiveness of the approaches to "Policy development and review" in this section and to review the course as a whole. Participants may wish to use their action planning sheets as the basis for these evaluations. The facilitator can collect these in to provide an indication of the success of the course as a whole. For further discussion of evaluation, see Appendix 3.

## ACTIVITY 2                            TASK

**I**   As a whole group you have generated a list of all the people/groups who might be interested in the school having a policy for "Race, Equality and Science Teaching". From this list enter in the segments of the circle below the six groups you collectively think it would be most important to consult when framing a policy, or those who might be most interested.

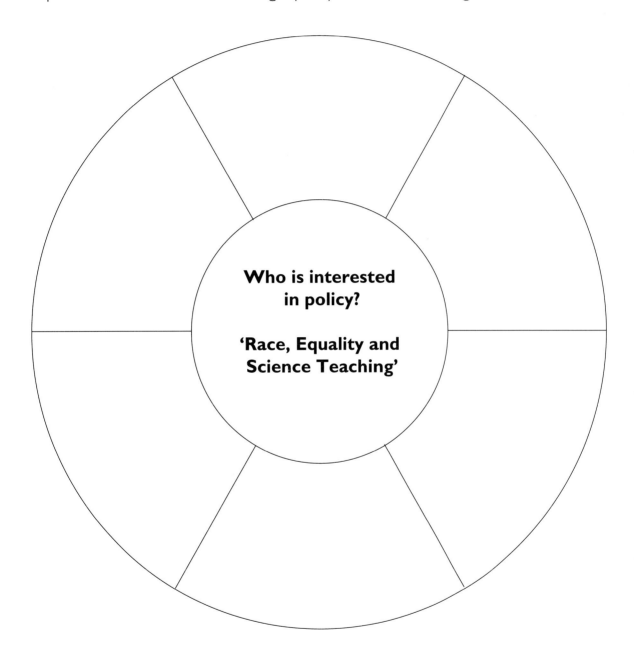

Now divide your group into pairs, each pair taking responsibility for two of the groups in your circle.

..................................................................................................................

**2** You have taken responsibility for two of the six 'interest groups' your group has prioritised. For each interest group enter the name into the centre of the circle and in the segments give up to four reasons why they would be interested in, or affected by, the policy on "Race, Equality and Science Teaching". These reasons can be positive or negative. You may wish to generate more than four and prioritise those you think are most important.

Each person will take responsibility for reporting back to your group on one of the interest groups and the reasons you decided upon.

**Group 1**

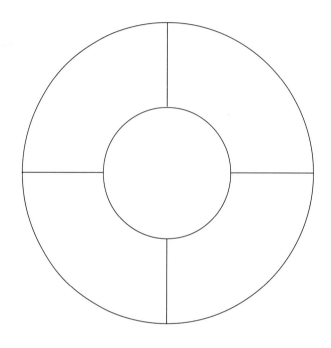

**Group 2**

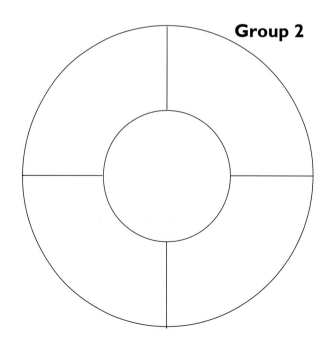

**ACTIVITY 4**                                                                    **TASK**

..........................................................................................

Each pair reports back their reasons to the whole group. Try to identify where the reasons for different groups are similar. Summarise the similarities by entering on the grid below and in each case write down all the interest groups for whom that reason (or a similar one) was given. Also enter the reasons which were not similar to any others and the interest group to which it was ascribed.

Choose one area of similarity and one different reason to report back on to the whole group.

| **Reason** | **Group(s) to whom it was ascribed** |
| --- | --- |
| | |

## SCENARIO A

You work in a large, multi-ethnic city primary school with 35% black developing bilingual pupils, 25% Afro-Caribbean, 40% white European and 5% other groups including Chinese and Vietnamese pupils. There are 15 teaching staff, including two Section 11 teachers and a community liaison teacher, plus several ancillary and classroom support workers.

The school has a policy on multicultural education and considers itself strong in the area of community and parental links. The science coordinator wishes to develop a science policy in the school as the existing schemes are out of date and do not reflect national developments or other policies in the school.

A meeting has been convened of members of staff – including one per year team – plus other key personel. These could possibly include: deputy head or headteacher; Section 11 support teachers, community liaison teacher, ancillary support worker, a science advisory teacher.

Number attending: 5–8 people.

## TASK

The group is to consider what issues/areas such a policy statement should cover and address, and to make a manageable and comprehensive list of these. A short presentation should be prepared which relates the list to the scenario and to issues of equality.

........................................................................................

## SCENARIO B

You work in a small, mainly white, Church of England school in a rural village. Recently a Gujerati-speaking family has moved into the village and one of their children attends the school. Two Chinese pupils have attended the school for a year. There are six teaching staff and parents often help in classrooms and act as ancillary helpers.

The Headteacher has recently been on a L.E.A. course on "Education for equality in predominantly white schools" and is anxious to review the school's recently written curriculum policy statements in the light of this. The governors have supported the head but have reminded the head that they "aim to maintain" the school's Christian ethos throughout the review. The staff have decided to review the science policy first as a curriculum area, to illustrate how elements of equality and anti-racism might be related more generally to the revised curriculum policies.

This first staff meeting is attended by the teaching staff, and one, or more, of the governors may also be present.

Present: 6–8 people.


## TASK

The group is to consider what issues/areas the revised curriculum policy statements should cover and address, and to make a manageable and comprehensive list of these. A short presentation should be prepared which relates the list to the scenario and to issues of equality.

## SCENARIO C

You work in a 8–13 Middle School situated in a medium-sized market town. Most (80%) of the pupils are white, English first language speakers with 20% black pupils. The majority of these are Panjabi-speaking pupils of Pakistani origin (although all are second or third generation in Britain), with a small number of black and mixed-race children whose fathers are American service personel from the nearby base. There are 20 teaching staff and several ancillary workers. One of the teachers is funded under Section 11 provision.

The school has an integrated curriculum in years 5 and 6, while in years 7 and 8 there is more subject specialism, although the coordinators do collaborate on planning. The team of subject coordinators has recommended that a school policy on 'multicultural' education should be developed and each coordinator is to consult with year teams and subject team colleagues.

This is the meeting called by the science coordinator to discuss issues and implications of such a policy for science teaching in the school. Colleagues present could include the science coordinator, deputy headteacher, teachers from year 5 and 6 teams; science teachers in year 7 and 8, section 11 teacher, etc.

Number present: 5–8

## TASK

The group is to consider what issues/areas such a policy statement should cover and address, and to make a manageable and comprehensive list of these. A short presentation should be prepared which relates the list to the scenario and to issues of equality.

········································································

## SCENARIO D

You work in a large secondary school in a 'mainly white' suburban area. There are a small number of Asian and Afro-Caribbean pupils – mainly from professional families. Teaching staff number around 65. The governors and management team, in producing the School Development Plan have identified an overall Equal Opportunities need. The initial impetus for this came from staff concerned with gender issues in the school, but in discussion the brief has been broadened to include Race. A general policy for equal opportunities is being developed by a Working Party and this group has requested that departments put the matter on the agenda for a department meeting where staff can suggest what the school's policy should address.

The head of science has called the meeting, and all science teachers have been asked to attend and contribute.

## TASK

The group is to consider what issues/areas such a policy statement should cover and address, and to make a manageable and comprehensive list of these. A short presentation should be prepared which relates the list to the scenario and to issues of equality.

## ACTIVITY I                                                          TASK

...............................................................................................

## SCENARIO E

You work in a multi-ethnic secondary school in the centre of a large town. A large proportion of the pupils at the school are black – mainly from Afro-Caribbean and Bangladeshi origin. However, a recent language survey has identified smaller numbers of pupils speaking a range of languages as a mother tongue including Turkish, Italian, Gujerati, Urdu, Polish, Vietnamese, Chinese and Greek.

The school has a policy on anti-racism, which is very much at the whole institutional level – addressing issues such as racist incidents, etc. However the recent survey has led the school to feel that it has not addressed curriculum-level issues of access and achievement. Each faculty has been asked to come up with specific recommendations in these areas.

At a science and technology faculty meeting, a range of colleagues are in attendance. These could possibly include:

head of faculty, technology coordinator, science coordinator, other teachers including probationers, a recently-appointed faculty postholder in Equal Opportunities (B allowance); a senior teacher head of year, a senior teacher, TVEI coordinator, etc.

## TASK

The group is to consider what issues/areas such a policy statement should cover and address, and to make a manageable and comprehensive list of these. A short presentation should be prepared which relates the list to the scenario and to issues of equality.

## SCENARIO F

You work in a F.E. college in a small county town which has a strong Chinese community and smaller, but significant, numbers of black families from various backgrounds.

The college does not operate any access courses, although this is something now being considered by senior management. This is partly due to a recent client survey which was set up to address declining numbers of students attending. The survey highlighted the fact that there were very few minority ethnic students attending the college.

Some members of the science and engineering department have initiated a wider informal review of their department's approach to minority ethnic students and the curriculum they are providing. At present, this has been set up as an interest group, and the first meeting is yet to take place. They have decided to discuss recommendations for policy change to the department and college managers to consider. The group is made up predominantly of young and junior staff, the exception being a lecturer who is second in biology and who has been at the college a number of years. Other staff members have been invited to attend, including the C.P.V.E. team leader and the vice principal who was responsible for the survey.

## TASK

The group is to consider what issues/areas they would wish such policy recommendations to cover and address, and to make a manageable and comprehensive list of these. A short presentation should be prepared which relates the list to the scenario and to issues of equality.

## MANAGING A ROLE PLAY OR SIMULATION: NOTES FOR PARTICIPANTS

Role play and simulation differ from other discussion strategies in that participants actively experience tasks and decision making in specific, simulated contexts. The reflection on those tasks, decisions and their process and outcomes takes place outside the role play or simulation through the preparation and de-briefing processes that are an essential part of any such activity.

We would not wish to make any signifigant distinction between role play and simulation, but whilst in role play you are usually asked to play a persona somewhat different from your own, in simulation participants are left free to adopt a persona which is more or less themselves, and it is the context and task which are simulated.

Effective role play and simulation demands very careful preparation. A clear brief is vital. You will need to be fully conversant with the situation or context within which you are operating as well as the beliefs and attitudes to be represented, together with the likely behaviour of the person being played. Not only do you need to portray the role's personality, but also how the person reconciles her/himself with the way in which s/he approaches her/his job. Sufficient time needs to be taken for this familiarisaiton and, in role play, for establishing in your mind a fully rounded personality for the role to be played.

It is difficult to avoid stereotypes, but it is essential to avoid caricatures. It is often helpful to imagine yourself to be a person you know quite well, someone you like and respect or admire. If you try to portray someone you dislike or despise, you are unlikely to do them justice and that will make it easy for other people to dismiss their views. In general, the creation of sympathetic roles is usually more helpful to the learning required by the participants than the creation of aggressive or overly intolerant roles.

As in simulation, it is not essential for role play to be based on briefs that have been supplied. It is interesting and effective for people to prepare their own briefs from broad guidelines. What is important is that roles are played consistently, and without lapse, until the pre-arranged time for de-briefing.

The de-briefing stage should allow you to reflect on the way your role has influenced the people and processes with which you have been engaged. It also allows reflection on why roles have been played the way they have. In the de-briefing of simulations, you will have the opportunity to reflect on the way you respond to, and deal with, situations and tasks.

We have also found role play to be very enlightening about the attitudes, experiences and feelings of others. You really can begin to experience how people think, feel and react. You can actually feel yourself getting angry about things which in real life you might think quite trivial. Indeed, one of the minor difficulties about role play is the problem of getting out of role in order to explore it from the point of view of one's real everyday self.

There are, of course, many differences between role playing and real life. For the purpose of these exercises, one important thing is that you have to invent reality as you go along. If you are questioned about, or have to react to, an issue which was not mentioned in your brief, you will have to invent an attitude quickly to cope with the situation. This, of course, is one reason why it is important to explore the role thoroughly in advance, in order to internalise some of its intrinsic attitudes. You will probably be surprised how easy it is to do this.

Finally we would like to mention the liberating aspect of role play. It enables you to explore attitudes and approaches with which you might have some sympathy, but would not risk in reality. After all, you can always reject them afterwards; you are not necessarily putting them forward as your own beliefs.

## STAGE 1: DISCUSSION

You have been assigned an issue to consider. Eventually you will prepare a statement on this issue to be included in the draft policy.

**a**  In your group consider your issue, using the "Cue cards", if necessary, and discuss these – affirming or rejecting the statements as appropriate. Add any of your own in the blank spaces. Come to a general agreement about what eventually might appear in your statement.

**b**  Then consider:

- who you may have to involve, or consult, in producing your statement, and when and how you will do this;

- what information you might need to get, and where might you get it from (don't forget other school policies or cross-curricular opportunities).

Prepare your lists for report back.

## STAGE 2: DISCUSSION

As a group, imagine that you have completed your consultation and information gathering exercise and are now ready to produce your statement.

**a**  First consider the kind of information and opinions that your enquiries may have elicited (e.g. what might various individuals and interest groups have said to you, what documentation might you have hadto work with, and so on?)

**b**  Then write your statement on your issues – which could be included in the whole group's overall policy – on a large sheet of paper, for report back, display and discussion.

# Cue cards on policy issues

---

## THE SCIENCE CURRICULUM

- should be relevant to all pupils regardless of class, gender and ethnicity;
- should reflect and build on the experiences of all pupils;
- should portray science as an everyday, human activity;
- should put science in cultural, historical, social, political, environmental and economic contexts;
- should be global in nature and portray positive images of people and places;
- should challenge racism and the false science which defines 'human race';
- should challenge deterministic arguments – particularly with regard to human behaviour and characteristics;
- should challenge all forms of stereotyping and discrimination.

---

## LANGUAGE POLICY

- should emphasise the importance of clear understanding in science for all pupils;
- should value linguistic diversity in the classroom and society, and positively build on pupils' language experiences;
- should ensure that collaborative and cooperative tasks are structured to ensure access and language development for all;
- should recognise the needs of developing bilingual pupils, and ensure that their learning is effectively supported in the classroom;
- should emphasise the responsibility of all teachers for the language development of their pupils.

## TEACHING AND LEARNING STYLES

- should be recognised as a major factor in providing access to the science curriculum for all children;
- should include a wide range of strategies, particularly those which are collaborative rather than competitive;
- should ensure that pupils' own experiences and viewpoints are valued and built on;
- should ensure that pupils' own ideas and assumptions are challenged;
- should enable pupils to share, with the teacher, control over the learning process;
- should enable pupils to develop autonomy and responsibility for their own learning;
- should enable pupils to be critical observers of the world around them and 'activists' in challenging injustice.

## POLICY IN ASSESSMENT AND ACHIEVEMENT

- should acknowledge that teacher expectations and treatment of pupils is a major factor in their achievement;
- should recognise that racism and discrimination are major factors in pupils' levels of achievement;
- should aim to eradicate cultural and other forms of bias from classroom resources and assessment materials, and to provide positive images for all pupils;
- should ensure that developing bilingual pupils are not denied access to the curriculum, or are unable to show what they know, understand and can do;
- should recognise that teaching styles, language issues and curriculum content and contexts are all factors in achievement;
- should aim to provide equality of access, opportunity and of outcome for all groups within the institution;
- should ensure systematic monitoring of achievement/vocational destination, etc. for all groups within the school or college.

## A WHOLE SCHOOL POLICY ON EQUALITY AND JUSTICE

- should be reflected in all other policies and should be known, understood and implemented by all members of, and in all teams or departments in, the school community;
- should include a clear commitment to equality and justice for all pupils, teachers and others in the school community;
- should include clear guidelines on behaviour, with specific opposition to racial and sexual harassment and how to deal with and challenge it, in school and community;
- should contain clear commitments to working with the whole community and promoting links with minority ethnic community groups, parents and other bodies;
- should deal specifically with issues of recruitment, retention and promotion of staff – particularly black teachers, women and those from minorities, to ensure equal opportunities in practice, and to provide positive role models for all pupils;
- should ensure that all governors and staff receive regular professional development and training in equality issues;
- should ensure that equality and justice issues are seen as ongoing priorities in the School or College Development Plan, and where resource allocation is concerned.

. . . . . . . . . . . . . . . . . . . . . . . . . . . . . . . . . . . . . . . . . . . . . . . . . . . . . . . . . . . . . . . . . . . . . . . . . . . . . . . . . . . . . . . . . . . . . . . . . . . .

**1** You have been assigned, or taken ownership of, an issue which forms an aspect of a policy on "Race, Equality and Science Teaching". In your group, discuss the question:

" Can the issue be broken down further into more specific areas for action?"

Generate a list of such areas for action and then prioritise three or four of these, and enter them onto the Task sheet 1 provided.

**2** Choose one of the areas of action prioritised above. Generate a list of strategies which you feel might be effective in addressing this in a school or college. Prioritise no more than three of these strategies and write them in the second column on Task sheet 2 provided.

(Note: you need not have three strategies, one or two good ones would be adequate if the group agrees.)

**3** For the strategies you have identified, your group is to discuss the question:

" How can we judge whether the strategy has worked, or is working? What are the criteria, or indicators, of success?"

Write these criteria and indicators in the third column on Task sheet 2.

(Note: you may wish to consider timescales, targets and whether the criteria and indicators can be measured statistically – i.e. they are quantitative – or whether they will be judged qualititively – through comments, documents, observations, behaviour, etc.)

Stages 2 and 3 could be repeated for your other "Areas for action" identified if required.

**4** You will now have a range of indicators and strategies which can be shared with the whole group.

# Guidance for running activities

1  Groups of 3–5 take on ownership of an issue, each of which is an identified aspect of a policy in "Race, Equality and Science Teaching". The group is asked to discuss the question "Can the issue be broken down into more specific areas for action?" A number of these are generated and then prioritised to three or four areas for action. These are then recorded on the first task sheet.

In the example below the teachers have taken the issue "Language in science" and following discussion have decided that there are three main areas of action which need addressing in isolation.

**1**  Valuing linguistic diversity
**2**  Bilingual pupils' needs
**3**  Language in existing resources

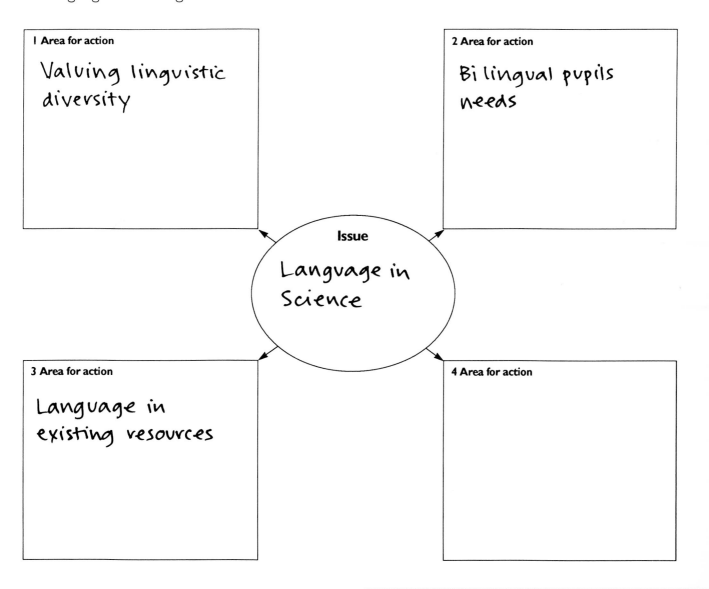

| 1 Area for action |
|---|
| Valuing linguistic diversity |

| 2 Area for action |
|---|
| Bilingual pupils needs |

**Issue**

Language in Science

| 3 Area for action |
|---|
| Language in existing resources |

| 4 Area for action |
|---|
| |

**2** For one area of action recorded on Task sheet 1, the group is asked to brainstorm a list of practical strategies which might be effective in addressing it in schools/colleges. These are then prioritised and no more than three strategies selected and entered on the flow chart below.

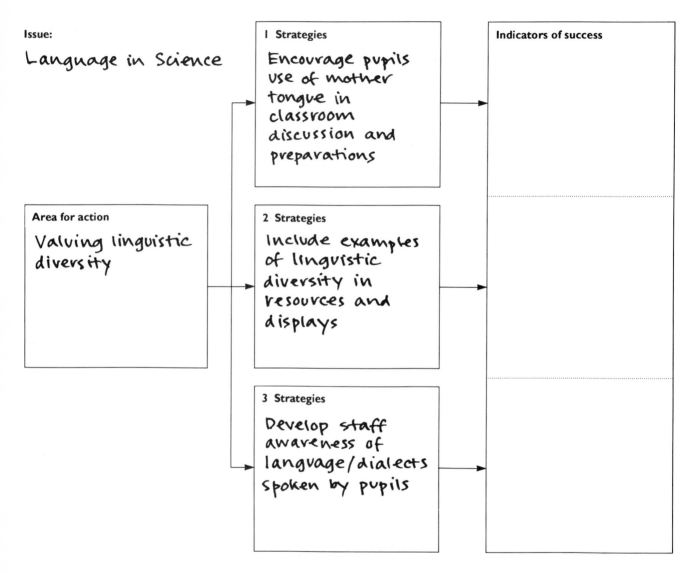

Issue:
**Language in Science**

Area for action
**Valuing linguistic diversity**

1 Strategies
**Encourage pupils use of mother tongue in classroom discussion and preparations**

2 Strategies
**Include examples of linguistic diversity in resources and displays**

3 Strategies
**Develop staff awareness of language/dialects spoken by pupils**

Indicators of success

**3** For the strategies identified, the group then discuss the question "How can we judge whether the strategy has worked, or is working? What are the criteria, or indicators, of success?" These are then entered in the final column of the flow chart on the second task sheet.

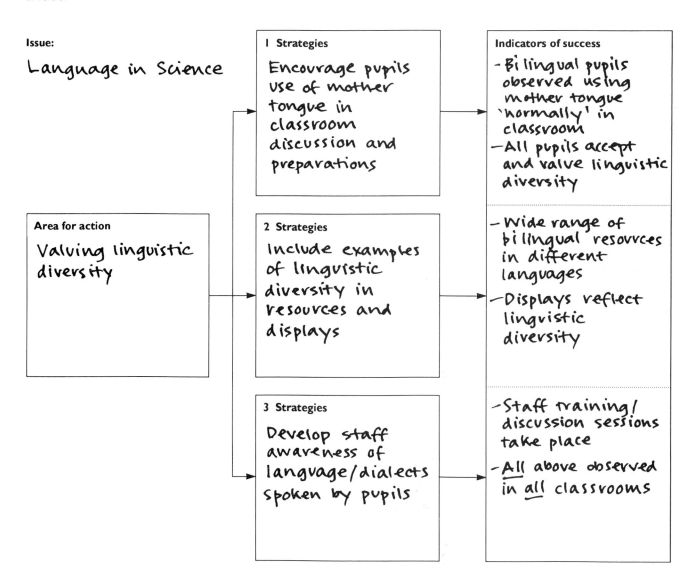

One further activity which might be useful for groups, is to analyse their indicators as quantitative (i.e. those that can be statistically measured and monitored), and qualitative (i.e. those which are not measured in numerical terms, but may be based on comments, documents, observations, etc.) Similar analysis can distinguish those indicators specific to science and race equality issues, from those which are more general.

# Pro forma 1

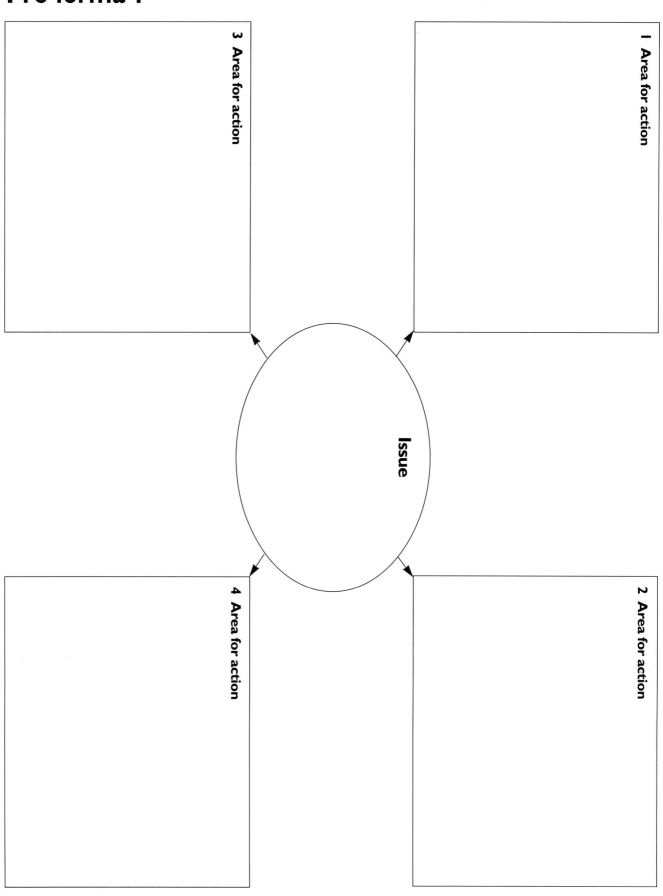

**3 Area for action**

**1 Area for action**

**Issue**

**4 Area for action**

**2 Area for action**

# Pro forma 2

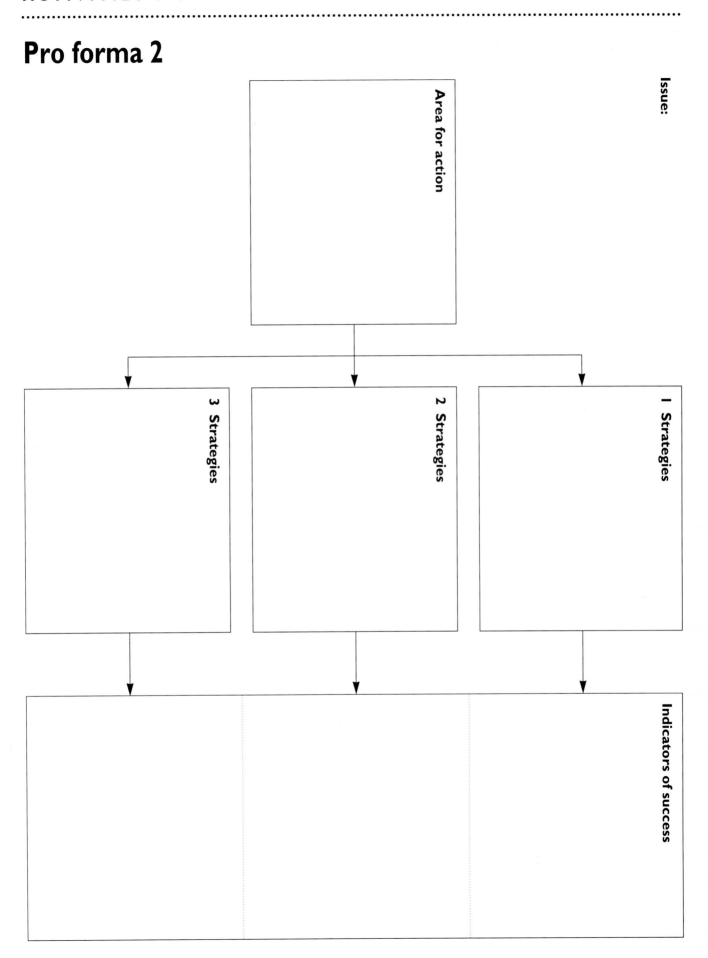

Issue:

Area for action

1 Strategies

2 Strategies

3 Strategies

Indicators of success

# Action planning sheet

| Issue | Where do I/we start? | What are my/our longerterm goals ? | How will I/we monitor and evaluate success? | Any other comments |
|---|---|---|---|---|
| 1 | | | | |
| 2 | | | | |
| 3 | | | | |
| 4 | | | | |

## AN AIDE-MEMOIRE FOR PLANNING CHANGE

Following this course:

- what issues are a priority for my own classroom and my own teaching?

- what issues are a priority for my team?

- what issues are a priority for my school/college?

- who are my allies in my team and institution?

- who will need convincing?

- who may act as 'barriers' to all or some, of these developments?

- are there other 'barriers'?

- what are my longer term goals?

- who will I share and develop these goals with?

- what are my strategies for implementing practical change in my classroom, my team and my school/college?

- how can I measure or evaluate the success of these strategies?

# Developing policy for equality

## A DISCUSSION PAPER

Before we embark on the processes of policy development, a number of questions must be asked: "How does a policy reflect the school or college and its community?"; "Is the insitution perceived as 'multicultural' or 'all-white'?"; "If we term it 'all-white' or 'mono-cultural', how sure are we that the description is accurate – and does it do justice to the variety of pupils and their backgrounds?".

If the institution is 'all-white' or 'predominantly white' in its intake and community, then the main focus of policy development is likely to be on the curriculum. In a primary school setting, it is likely that issues of equality will be considered in the context of the whole curriculum with the science coordinator playing a key role in cross-referencing contexts and perspectives in the light of National Curriculum and School Development Plan requirements. In a secondary school or college, the focus is more likely to be specifically scientific, and based within the department or faculty. In either case, the management of effective and necessary curricular change is crucial. Issues to address include: the nature of science and its wider social, economic and environmental contexts; the portrayal of science as a global, inter-cultural and everyday activity – both now and in history; racist bias in resource materials; positive images for all pupils; attitudes and behaviour of pupils, teachers and others in the school or college community.

All the above apply equally in a multicultural environment – even if there are only a few individual black and/or bilingual pupils – but other issues will also apply more specifically. These will include: achievement; access to the whole curriculum (and to high-status courses in secondary schools and colleges); support for developing bilingual pupils in their learning; racial harassment, etc. In many of these areas, quantitative monitoring may need to take place to ensure that quality of access is reflected in the learning outcomes (and vocational and career destinations) of all pupils.

In all institutions, regardless of intake, a policy should be overtly reflected in the ethos of the school or college – that is a commitment to equality is made manifest in all areas of school or college life, and is understood by the whole community. Likewise, 'learning' issues such as teaching and learning styles, will have a direct bearing on the success or otherwise of implementing policy. Put simply, in all phases issues such as racism and 'science in society' are more likely to be successfully addressed in an open student-centred learning approach. Similarly using a range of teaching and learning styles will enhance access to the curriculum for *all* pupils, including those from minority groups or who are bilingual. In a primary, school it may be easier to ensure common experiences throughout the curriculum; whereas in secondary schools and colleges the whole-school view on equality and learning issues needs to be clearly structured across departments or faculties.

In this context then, a multicultural or anti-racist policy cannot be separated from the insitution's overall policies and ethos, whilst a specific policy on 'science for equality' (for example in a school science department) cannot be separated from whole-institution commitments to equality. An effective learning institution is, therefore, one which makes manifest its commitment to equality in all areas of activity; 'multicultural' approaches developed in isolation from the overall institutional development cannot be ultimately effective.

## THE POLICY

The policy itself may be:

• a statement of intent for a school or department;
• a consensus of 'values' validated by a range of people working within a school or department;
• based on the views of teachers, governors, non-teaching staff, pupils/students, parents, community groups, L.E.A., D.E.S., etc.;
• appropriate to a particular institution or department.

The policy might include reference to issues such as:

• access to the (science) curriculum and different courses;
• the needs of bilingual pupils/students;
• behaviour and racial harassment;
• attitudes of staff and pupils regarding prejudices and stereotypes;
• curriculum content and contexts;
• teaching and learning styles;
• staff recruitment and development;
• home and community links.

The process and people involved in developing a policy can be summarised as below. It will be useful to come to some collective views as to the answers to the questions posed in the diagram before embarking on the process itself.

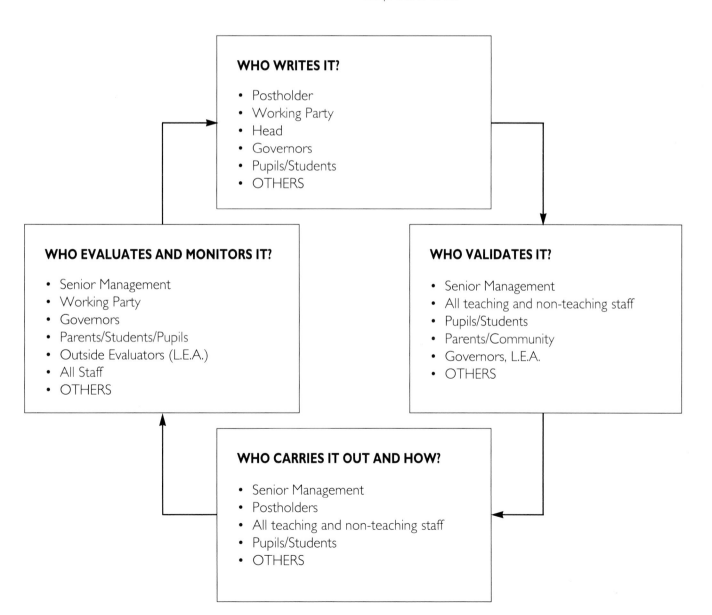

**WHO WRITES IT?**

• Postholder
• Working Party
• Head
• Governors
• Pupils/Students
• OTHERS

**WHO EVALUATES AND MONITORS IT?**

• Senior Management
• Working Party
• Governors
• Parents/Students/Pupils
• Outside Evaluators (L.E.A.)
• All Staff
• OTHERS

**WHO VALIDATES IT?**

• Senior Management
• All teaching and non-teaching staff
• Pupils/Students
• Parents/Community
• Governors, L.E.A.
• OTHERS

**WHO CARRIES IT OUT AND HOW?**

• Senior Management
• Postholders
• All teaching and non-teaching staff
• Pupils/Students
• OTHERS

## THE CYCLE OF INSTITUTIONAL CHANGE AND DEVELOPMENT

A model which may be useful in considering the processes of change in a school or department with regard to equality issues is shown in the diagram below. It puts the policy statement – here seen as a statement of intent – at the centre of the cycle, but regards the other aspects – the processes themselves – as equally important. When dealing with equality issues to do with 'race', it is crucial that the 'Raising issues' initial stage is adequately dealt with through INSET activities similar to those contained in this manual.

Issues to address at this initial stage include looking at the nature of science and its relationship with society; the nature of society, and in particular its multicultural and multi-ethnic nature; the nature of racism and how it manifests itself in society, particularly in science and education; the nature of science education itself – what do we hope to achieve through teaching science?

In the later stages, monitoring and evaluating key indicators and criteria will be important; these may be qualitative or quantiative in nature, but in any case will be specific to an institution and the group of pupils and community it serves. The cycle below is a process model for developing and implementing policy, which is reflected in the workshop activities contained in this manual.

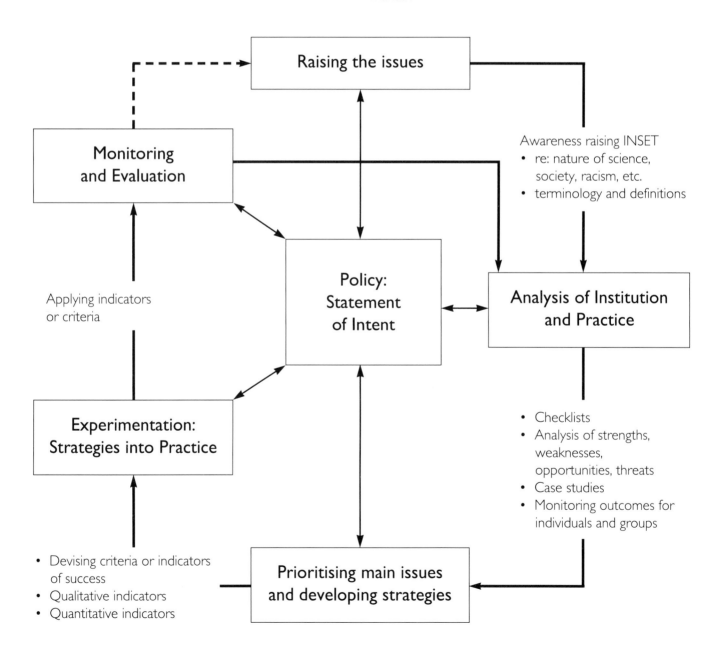

# A discussion paper

· · · · · · · · · · · · · · · · · · · · · · · · · · · · · · · · · · · · · · · · · · · · · · · ·

This paper was prepared for the ASE by the ASE
Multicultural Education Working Party for discussion prior
to formulating a policy in 1990/91.

## SECTION I    INTRODUCTION

**1.1**  The Working Party emphasises the potential of science
to enhance the curriculum by drawing on the richness and
diversity of cultures and on their practice of science, now and
throughout history. We also wish to emphasise the powerful
role of science teaching for combating racism and prejudice in
society.

**1.2**  In particular a science curriculum is required which can
help prepare all young people for:
• life in our culturally diverse society in which there is systematic discrimination directed against some of its groups (1);
• an awareness of the complex relationships and inequalities
between and within nations (2, 3);
• the increasing interdependence between peoples in the
world (4).
All this will involve addressing the nature and contexts of
science, racism at all levels in education and devising strategies
for providing genuine access to science for children from all
groups in our society (5).

**1.3**  The Working Party believes that the issues of racism and
access to the curriculum for all children in a multicultural
society need to be addressed as a matter of urgency. By its
very nature, racism aims to devalue specific groups of human
beings based on the colour of skin and/or cultural and social
background. If an entitlement to a balanced and relevant
science curriculum (as, for example, stated in the National
Curriculum for England and Wales) is to be taken up by every
child, there must be recognition that in establishing equality of
opportunity, racism will always have a negative effect on children's learning, achievement and attitudes towards others (6).

**1.4**  We believe that a science curriculum which ignores the
above issues will disadvantage *all* children: white children
because of the impediment caused by their unchallenged
assumptions and attitudes they hold about the black and
other minority communities (4); and children from black and
other minority groups because their progress will be impeded
by inequalities in their access to science provision (5).
Furthermore, all children will be denied the enrichment
brought to science by the multicultural dimension (7).

**1.5**  The language surrounding the issues of multiculturism
and 'race' are sometimes emotive, and quite often mean
different things to different people. So that our message is
unequivocal, we have tried to discuss what we mean by
certain key terms in Appendix 2.

## SECTION 2    THE CONTEXT OF SCIENCE EDUCATION

**2.1**  We believe that science has sometimes been practised in
a way that reflects discrimination in our society. Far from
always reflecting an 'objective reality', science has on occasions
been used to justify racist practices (8). The concept of
'human race' is itself an example of this process; pseudo-
scientific theories which divided humanity into distinct 'racial'
types were used to justify social and political policies in the
U.S.A., European colonies and Britain. It is only recently that
these theories have been discarded, although references to
'racial types' can still be found in some older science text
books and other sources (9). The Working Party asserts that
the concept of 'human race' has no scientific validity but is a
social and historical concept which all teachers of science have
a duty to challenge (8, 10, 11).

**2.2**  Science and scientific discovery is often portrayed in the
media and in school texts as the preserve of white men in
Western societies. In fact, people from all cultures are and
have always been involved in scientific exploration and
discovery (12).

**2.3**  Science is a human activity, and consequently scientific
ideas are developed in a cultural and a socio-political context
influenced by the values and institutions of that culture.
Science and scientists are therefore unlikely to be 'neutral'.
The study of 'The Nature of Science' provides opportunities
for investigating this aspect of scientific activity and how
different cultures contribute to the development of scientific
ideas (see, eg. 13, 14).

**2.4**  When examples of non-Western contributions to
scientific understanding are given in school they tend to
concentrate upon isolated 'discoveries' from the past. It is
important to recognise that different societies have viewed
science in different ways. For example, science has been much
more an integral part of people's day-to-day lives, daily

practices and religion in many societies, as against the marked separation between science, religion and culture in other parts of the world. Present-day examples used to illustrate science operating in non-Western cultures should not simply focus upon 'appropriate' technology in 'Third World' countries; if these are the only images presented to children they may reinforce stereotypes. Examples of 'high' and 'low' technologies should be used to illustrate universal principles and should be drawn from a variety of situations and places (15).

**2.5** It is important that science is taught in its human, social, cultural and environmental contexts, and there are related issues which cannot be ignored if science education is to be a positive force in tackling racism and raising children's awareness. These will include the effect of science and technology upon people around the world and upon their environment. The political, industrial and economic pressures which often dictate the priorities for research also need to be addressed (see, e.g. 16, 17, 18, 19).

## SECTION 3   CHALLENGING RACISM

**3.1** It is widely accepted that effective teaching and learning in science depends upon children's motivation and commitment. This in turn depends upon:
• children's self esteem and the way in which their ideas and their cultural backgrounds are valued and used by the teacher;
• teacher expectations;
• the challenging and dispelling of stereotypes – whether cultural, racial or social.(see, e.g. 20, 21, 22).

**3.2**   When placing science within a human context care should be taken to make sure visual images presented to children in books, posters and other materials provide positive images of people from all cultures. It is important that there should be role models for all children in our multicultural society. Stereotypical and negative images must be avoided as should, for example, the 'structured absence' of black people from resources and texts (23, 24).

**3.3** It is important to choose topics and materials which both reflect a multicultural perspective and which directly challenge stereotyping and racism. In the earlier years this may be done through topics such as 'Ourselves' (25), and through approaches to science and technology which assess the appropriateness of technologies and their implications for people and the planet. At any age, we prefer environmental and global approaches, rather than a possibly demeaning focus on 'Third World Development' issues (26). Themes which

encompass genetics and human variation should also directly contribute to an anti-racist curriculum.

**3.4** The processes of science offer unique opportunities for children to explore critically their own viewpoints and those of others, and teachers of science can help in challenging prejudice directly (27). Teachers need to recognise and to deal firmly and consistently with all forms of racial abuse; teachers themselves should avoid making stereotypical judgements and expectations on a pupil's performance.

**3.5** Although good teaching can tackle racism, it is most effective when performed within the context of whole school or department policy. These policies should provide strategies which seek to eliminate all forms of racism and should set out clear procedures for dealing with racist incidents. Issues of access should also be addressed, particularly those which affect science options, groupings, language policy, etc. (28, 29).

## SECTION 4   EQUALITY OF ACCESS

**4.1**   Recent curriculum statements (notably the National Curriculum in England and Wales) include statements of entitlement and access to science for all children irrespective of their cultural or social background. Everyone involved needs to recognise the many factors affecting access to science; the quality of access establishes for children from different backgrounds the potential for success or underachievement (30, 31).

### Language

**4.2**   Clear understanding is of foremost importance in learning science. It is important that the diversity of linguistic and scientific experiences of pupils is properly valued and built on. This diversity includes pupils who operate effectively in a range of languages and language forms such as Bengali, Chinese, Gaelic, Polish, Punjabi, Urdu, Welsh, etc. – as well as regional and cultural dialects (32, 33).

**4.3** The specialised use of vocabulary in science can be a barrier to understanding; even terms such as 'energy' and 'animal' have both everyday and scientific meanings. We recognise that science is also an important vehicle for language development and that acquisition of 'scientific language' is essential in achieving success in science. At the same time, teachers recognise that it is important to introduce new concepts with a familiar vocabulary and in a familiar and appropriate context (24, 34).

**4.4** Teachers need to use pupil talk and discussion as an essential starting point for pupils' conceptual development of science. For bilingual learners pupil talk is a crucial element in their linguistic and conceptual development.

**4.5** Further barriers to learning science are created for some pupils (particularly so for those who are building a competency in standard English) by requiring them to use impersonal and passive styles in report writing. More intimate, familiar and no less valid alternatives to traditional written forms of reporting include collaborative work, shared writing, annotated drawings, posters and models. These strategies allow all pupils to present their findings as well as demonstrate their understanding and further extend their skills of written language(33).

**4.6** The issues considered above have implications for resource materials. These materials should be appropriate and made accessible to all pupils and be suitably differentiated. This does not mean the simplification of language, but for some children it may be helpful to provide parallel material (whether in English or bilingual format), which may require input from specialist support and advisory colleagues (33, 35).

## Teaching Strategies

**4.7** The use of a wide range of learning strategies will also help in promoting access for all pupils. For example, process-based science approaches, collaborative and active learning techniques (which are particularly familiar aspects in good primary practice) and setting the science taught in appropriate contexts will help in all phases to achieve a climate which values and builds upon pupils' ideas and experiences and so assists equality of access. Promoting and enabling pupils in individual and collective decision making can also contribute positively to an ethos of equality (36).

## Support in Classrooms

**4.8** Support for individual black and/or bilingual pupils (where this is required) is likely to be through 'Section 11' funded teachers. We strongly favour forms of in-class support where the class and support teachers work collaboratively. Indeed, in our view, regular withdrawal is likely to lead to social isolation and labelling, which further impedes access to the curriculum and is discriminatory in nature. Class and support teachers therefore need to work together and the support provided should be regularly reviewed to maintain and monitor effectiveness. If no such support is available, teachers may wish to seek advice or support from their Local Education Authority (37, 38).

## Assessment

**4.9** It is clear that assessment has profound implications for pupils who could be disadvantaged by procedures which contain linguistic or cultural bias. Some children may need assessment in their mother tongue – the key objective being that a pupil is able to fully understand any task set. On the other hand a pupil may be seriously disadvantaged if assessment is undertaken in a language different from the teaching and learning which precedes it. This implies the need for a bilingual mode of teaching and assessment, even though it has major resource implications (39).

**4.10** In any assessment, the administrator's expectation of pupils may affect the ways questions are asked and tasks presented. Great care must be taken to forestall the effects of expectations which stem from racial and cultural assumptions (and those arising from gender and social class). Children must not be inhibited in showing what they genuinely know, understand and can do.

## Whole School Issues

**4.11** Other factors which affect access will include: the way pupils and students are allocated to groups in classroom, school and college; arrangements for home-school and community links and, in secondary and further education sectors, expectations of pupils and students during careers counselling. These will all have an effect on young people accessing science-based careers or further study (40, 41).

## Staff

**4.12** The importance of black teachers in schools cannot be underestimated. While providing role models for black pupils they will help to reduce the negative and racist experiences of some pupils which can affect their future career patterns, not least those who might otherwise enter teaching.

**4.13** Black teachers are under-represented in the profession and even fewer achieve middle and senior management educational posts. We would stress the importance of positive recruitment strategies for teacher education and that institutions of higher education address the issues of educational access for all potential teachers who, while qualified in most respects, may not fulfil some certain institutional requirements (42, 43, 44).

**4.14** We would stress the importance of professional development of all staff in all educational establishments through the development and implementation of policies which ensure equal opportunities.

**SECTION 5   CONCLUSION**

**5.1**  The Working Party suggests that individual science teachers will be most effective in addressing the issues raised in this document when supported by a whole school or department multicultural policy – where this exists. Where it does not, they should be pro-active in influencing their department and school toward the development of a policy. The Working Party's view is that the beginning of policy development is likely to be at classroom level, with teachers of science starting to engage all who are connected with the school – other staff, governors, parents, and children. Governers in particular will need to be fully aware of the reasons for development in this area, as they will be responsible under L.M.S. for determining resource priorities. Related INSET should involve staff and governors.

**5.2**  Although equality of access may be monitored by reviewing achievement levels, examination results and the career destinations of children, other aspects are equally important, if harder to monitor. These include the attitudes of children, and staff and the school's relationship with parents and the community.

**5.3**  The Working Party believes that the Association for Science Education has a particularly important role to fulfil in clarifying multicultural issues for teachers of science. We hope that this document will begin this process.

November 1990

# References

1  Swann (1985)  **Education for All**  Chapter 2  London: HMSO

2  DES (1977)  **Education in Schools**  London: HMSO

3  Lewis J, Kelly P (eds)  **Science and Technology Education and Future Human Needs**  Vol. 1  London: Pergamon Press

4  Swann (1985)  op.cit. 1  Chapter 3

5  Maughan B and Rutter M (1986)  Black pupils' progress in secondary schools: 11 Examination attainment  **British Journal of Developmental Psychology**  4 pp19-29

6  DES (1989)  **Science in the National Curriculum**  London: HMSO

7  Swann (1985)  op.cit. 1  Chapter 4 par 3.44

8  UNESCO (1983)  **Racism, Science and Pseudoscience**  Paris: UNESCO

9  Monger G (ed) (1975)  **Revised Nuffield Biology: The Perpetuation of Life**  Book 4 p18  London: Longman Group

10  Verma G, Ashworth B (1986)  **Ethnicity and Educational Acheivement in British Schools**  Chapter 2  London: Macmillan

11  DES (1989)  op.cit. 6  Non-statutory guidance  Section F

12  Craft A, Klein C (1986)  **Agenda for Multicultural Teaching**  Section 23  York: Longman for SCDC

13  Martins J (1987)  **The History of Science and Technology**  London: North London Science Centre

14  Needham J (1979)  **The Grand Titration**  London: George Allen and Unwin

15  Waddington D (ed) (1987)  **Education, Industry and Technology**  Science and Technology and Future Human Needs  Vol. 3  Oxford; Pergamon

16  Kirwan D F (ed) (1987)  **Energy Resources in Science Education**  Science and Technology and Future Human Needs  Vol. 7  Oxford: Pergamon

17  Baez A (ed) (1987)  **The Environment and Science and Technology Education**  Science and Technology and Future Human Needs  Vol. 8  Oxford: Pergamon

18  Frazer M J, Kornhauser A (eds) (1987)  **Ethics and Social Responsibility in Science Education**  Science and Technology and Future Human Needs  Vol 2  Oxford: Pergamon

19  Kelly P, Lewis J (eds) (1987)  **Education and Health**  Science and Technology and Future Human Needs  Vol. 5  Oxford: Pergamon

20  Rutter M et al (1979)  **Fifteen Thousand Hours**  London: Open Books

21  Eggleston J et al (1986)  **Education for Some**  Stoke: Trentham Books

22  Kelly A (1987)  'Who gets Science Education?'  Paper prepared for British Sociological Society Conference, University of Leeds

23  Ditchfield C (ed) (1987)  **Better Science: Working for a Multicultural Society**  Curriculum Guide 7  London: Heineman Educational Books / Association for Science Education for the School Curriculum Development Committee

24  Sutton C (ed) (1981)  **Communicating in the Classroom**  Chapter 7  London: Hodder and Stoughton

25  DES (1987)  **Primary Schools: Some Aspects of Good Practice**  London: HMSO

26  Turner S, Turner A (1989)  'An international dimension to the teaching of science - opportunities in the National Curriculum'  **Multicultural Teaching**  Vol. 8 No.1

27  Brandt G (1986)  **The Realisation of Anti-Racist Teaching**  Falmer Press

28  Dastagir H (1986)  'A science department's in-service approach'  ILEA  **Multiethnic Review**  Vol. 5 No.2

29  Peacock A (1990)  'Building a multicultural dimension into primary science'  **Primary Sciences Review**  12

30  DES (1988)  **Science for Ages 5 to 16**  par 7.12-7.17  London: HMSO

31  Wright C (1986) in Eggleston J (1986)  op.cit. 21  Chapter 8

32  Davis F, Green T (1984)  **Reading for Learning in Science**  Edinburgh: Oliver and Boyd

33  Roach T, Smith D and Vasquez M (1990)  **Language and Learning in the National Curriculum: Bilingual Pupils and Secondary Science**  Hounslow: Schools Language Centre

34  Osborne R, Freyberg P (1985)  **Learning in Science: The Implications of Childen's Science**  Auckland: Heinemann

35  Sutton C (ed) (1981)  op.cit. 24

36  CLISP (1988)  **'CLIS in the Classroom'**  Leeds: CSSME

37  HMI (1984)  **Slow Learning and Less Successful Pupils in Secondary Schools**  London: DES

38  HMI (1990)  **Aspects of Primary Education - The Teaching and Learning of Science**  London: HMSO

39  DES (1988)  **National Curriculum - Task Group on Assessment and Testing - A report**  London: DES

40  Kelly A (1987)  op cit 27; Wright C (1986)  op.cit. 31

41  see Egglestone J (1986)  op.cit. 21

42  DES (1988)  **Ethnically Based Statistics on School Teachers**  Circular 8/89 (April)

43  University of London Institute of Education (1988)  **Opportunity for All:** Report of a conference on Recruitment into Teacher Education of students from the Black Communities and other ethnic minority groups  London: Institute of Education

44  Romger C (1988)  **Ethnic Minority Schoolteachers: a Survey**  Commission for Racial Equality

# Terms used in this manual: meaning and use

## INTRODUCTION

Any attempt to define terms when discussing issues of racism is fraught with difficulty. There will always be someone who will argue that your definition is wrong – or that a term should not be used. Terms for people, places, groups and concepts are always problematic in that they can become exclusive and inflexible labels. At best they then cease to be useful in any meaningful way, at worst they can perpetuate stereotypes and reinforce the very inequalities we hope to challenge! Despite this, we feel that it is important that those using the manual know where the writers are collectively 'coming from' and the standpoint that we have taken in writing and preparing these materials. To illustrate the difficulty, previous draft versions of a glossary caused quite fundamental disagreements within the Working Party when first published in our draft discussion pack "Race, Equality and Science Teaching" in January 1991! This attempt may be seen more as a set of discussions than definitions, nevertheless we hope that teachers will find it useful as background to this training package and as a focus for (more) active discussion.

## RACE

This is a term once applied in science to groups of interbreeding organisms with superficial features in common. Observable physical differences were used to separate organisms – including humans – into races (e.g. by skin or hair colour). The word 'race' in human terms was, however, often applied arbitrarily. For example it could refer to the whole of humankind – 'the human race' – or to goegraphical groups, nations, tribes or even families! The effect was to create stereotyping of groups by 'racial characteristics' – and for many years in this century the received wisdom has been that there are a number (variable!) of clearly defined, human racial types. The concept of 'Race', as applied to humans, has now been shown to have no scientific validity – genetic variation between geographic populations is statistically negligible compared with the variation between all human individuals, and we would argue that 'race' was a social construct used primarily to justify discriminatory practices.

## RACISM

Is the institutional force by which groups of people are discriminated against because of their 'race', colour of skin, culture, ethnicity, etc. In its contemporary forms, racism was born out of the 'science' of 'race' which defined non-white, non-'European' peoples as different and inferior, and as having definable characteristics. Such 'evidence' was then used to justify racist practices in many forms – colonialism, slavery, apartheid, genocide – as well as more subtle forms of discrimination. Racism is often used to describe discrimination at the levels of institution and society as opposed to individual prejudice or racialism, which refers to an individual's beliefs and behaviour.

## ANTI-RACIST/MULTICULTURAL EDUCATION

These are both approaches to education which aim to provide equality of opportunity to all children and students.

Their underlying philosophies differ however. Multicultural Education tends to recommend approaches to teaching which encourage positive representation of the variety of cultural and ethnic groups in society in all schools, in order to reduce prejudice and improve self-image and achievement of minority ethnic pupils. Anti-racism is concerned primarily with actively challenging institutional racism at all levels in education – but has often been seen as promoting action at the institutional, rather than classroom level. It is, by nature, oppositional and provides support and encouragement to students in recognising and opposing racism themselves. Some educationalists argue that the two approaches are mutually exclusive, others see successful practice emerging from both. Both are labels which may have outlived their usefulness; other terms such as 'education for equality and justice' have been advocated as a means of combining positive elements of both, at both classroom and institutional level.

## BLACK

This term is most often used in a positive sense by Black people themselves to denote solidarity and a common experience and resistance to racism. In this political sense, 'Black' refers to those who are challenging systems, in society and in institutions, which discriminate against them because they are not 'white'. It is sometimes used to describe African and Afro-Caribbean people, as distinct from Asian, but this use is rejected by many people from these groups who use 'Black' as a positive self-definition in the sense described above. In these publications we use 'Black' in this positive sense to indicate that children and students are not 'victims' to be 'helped', but 'people' to be 'empowered' in their classrooms and communities. There are some people who are subject to racism who will not define themselves as Black – these may include, for example, people from Chinese and Vietnamese, Jewish and Traveller communities. They may define themselves by their ethnicity, cultural characteristics or lifestyle – in all cases, self-definition is advocated and should be respected. On no account should the term 'coloured' be used – it implies exclusivity (i.e. white people are not 'coloured'), denies identity (by negatively labelling whole groups of people), and it has implications with regard to official racist usage in countries like South Africa.

## ETHNICITY

This is a relatively recent term which enables all people to define themselves by distinct geographical, cultural, linguistic and/or religious origins. In contrast to the stress on common experience denoted by the term 'Black', ethnicity denotes a distinct common 'origin' or 'identity' which can refer to a group or community – irrespective of the variety of lifestyles that might be found within it – and its place in a 'multi-ethnic' society. In educational terms, ethnicity can be used to define the specific needs and experiences which a child may have and which the educational system should be addressing, for example, particular manifestations of racism in a community, developing bilingualism, etc. Other similar terms have been used to 'define' groups of people – 'ethnic' is a label

## TERMS USED IN THIS MANUAL (CONTINUED)

sometimes used in right-wing tracts to denote all those who differ (in terms of culture, origin, language and skin colour) from the 'indiginous, white' group – we would reject this usage as exclusive and racist. The term 'ethnic minority' is commonly used to describe relative numerical membership of groups in society. Here 'white' people would be seen as belonging to an 'ethnic group' but the 'ethnic minorities' are those, mainly non-white, groups whose historical origins and culture are 'different' from the majority. Hence the term can be demeaning – especially if applied to an individual – and it still labels people as 'others'.

### MINORITY ETHNIC

Because it is an adjectival term, this term may avoid this labelling problem, whilst providing a useful way of describing to those in society, and in education, who may have specific experiences and needs which arise from their 'ethnicity'. Although we have (along with a number of writers in the field of equality) used this term in this publication, we have done so with some misgivings – it is clumsy and still contains the word 'ethnic' as a label, which as pointed out above, is often used in a negative sense.

### SECTION 11 (ELEVEN)

This is one of those shorthand pieces of jargon which everyone who works with minority ethnic children understands (or thinks they do!), but many others do not. Its origins lie in the Local Government Act of 1974, wherein "Section 11" provides the legal and financial framework for meeting the special needs for 'immigrant' communities from the New Commonwealth and Pakistan residing in Britain. Funding is provided from the Home Office and criteria for supporting such communities has been adjusted over the years. Although the underlying thrust of Section 11 has been to 'assimilate' or 'integrate' Black people into 'British' society, funding from Section 11 has, (in education at least), been used more creatively and positively, and many L.E.A.s have developed Multicultural and/or Anti-racist policy and practice through Section 11, as well as funding English as a Second Language teaching and other support. Recent Home Office changes have narrowed the focus once again and, from April 1992, such 'cultural' aspects of education will not be able to funded from this source. In many multi-ethnic schools, support teachers for minority ethnic pupils will be funded through Section 11.

### CULTURE

This is one of the most difficult terms to define. Terms like 'multicultural' and 'cultural diversity' are used freely without any clear understanding of what the 'culture' referred to actually means. Often it is only used to refer to 'other cultures', meaning those groups whose ethnicity and lifestyle is different from that the 'indiginous, white' population (who are assumed to share a homogenous culture). Many right wing writers now use 'culture', rather than the discredited concept of 'race' in this way as the benchmark of 'difference', and of who belongs in Britain. We regard culture as something more complex, dynamic and positive than this narrow and racist usage. Culture can be considered to be the social, artistic and spiritual manifestations of personal, group, community and national identity. It may be that people who consider they have a common 'ethnicity' will also share aspects of a common culture, but other factors such as gender, age, class, sexual orientation, peer group, region, belief, lifestyle, job, the media, etc. are as important in defining the culture(s) of individuals, communities or, indeed, of society as a whole. Britain, therefore, is a multicultural society, not simply because of the presence of black, minority ethnic groups, but due to the rich variety of cultural manifestations which exist throughout society – to which Black people and others positively contribute.

### "THIRD WORLD"

A label which many people find offensive in that it implies a 'third class' status for countries and peoples. It lends itself to easy stereotyping, avoiding the need to examine relative inequalities in development and the reasons for these. 'Under-developed country' is similarly negative and demeaning and 'developing country', although less negative still assumes a Western definition of development as industrial and implies that some countries (i.e. the West) have got there and are now 'developed'. The reality is that development is a process which occurs in all countries! 'Rich' and 'poor' may be generally accurate in descriptive terms, but they ignore inequalities within all nations and lead to stereotyping of people. The same applies to 'North' and 'South', and these terms are so general that they are of little practical use. In short, no shorthand 'label' for groups of countries is really satisfactory – yet, for writing purposes, shorthand is sometimes needed. In this publication we have compromised. We have tried to avoid generalist labels for countries where possible, and refer to specific countries by name. However where some shorthand is required we have used 'Third World' with our very clear misgivings indicated by the quote marks, on the grounds that it is a commonly understood term, and does convey, to some degree, the inequalities that undoubtedly exist between nations – which are, after all, modern manifestations of colonialist exploitation and racism.

# Evaluating the workshops

Evaluation is an essential part of any INSET activity and it is recommended that facilitators finish each session with an evaluative exercise. The purposes of evaluation can be summarised as:

• to assess how effective a particular exercise has been in meeting the needs of participants and addressing the stated purposes/aims of the workshop. This will provide an opportunity for participants to comment on the processes and materials used, and enable the facilitator to further improve, adapt or change these (if necessary) in the future.

• to plan future directions for training in this area. Each individual will respond to the workshops in a different way. For some, issues will be raised which they feel are important and which they wish to follow up. Others may be less clear about their future needs, but a reflective, evaluative activity may help participants to clarify their own viewpoints. In either case, the facilitator will find such feedback invaluable in planning future units and in determining which workshops will be best received and most effective.

Many INSET facilitators using the materials in this manual will already have their own evaluation processes – and these can be adapted for any of the workshops or sections. However a sample evaluation sheet is enclosed which facilitators are free to copy or adapt. The five sections on the sheet refer to:

**I** evaluating the success of the workshop against the stated purpose. It might be useful to type/write out the purpose onto the sheet as a reference for participants;

**2** an evaluation of the support materials provided with each workshop. Although every attempt has been made to ensure that the contexts, case studies and other materials are relevant, and drawn directly from classroom practice, in certain circumstances participants may feel that this is not the case. Their comments can lead to further refinement of the materials in future use.

**3** and **4** asking participants to identify important issues emerging, and then to consider which of these they would like to follow up, or find out more about. These important sections will enable the facilitator to plan further training and to base such plans on the needs and viewpoints of participants, as well as on her/his own assessment;

**5** more general evaluation referrring not just to content, but to a number of other factors which affect whether a course is successful or not. These will include the style of presentation, processes used, levels of intervention, etc. – as well as such items as the domestic arrangements, suitability and comfort of the accomodation, and so on. These more general comments should be welcomed, as they often highlight successes, and failures, which might not otherwise be perceived by the facilitator. Hhere we would like to stress the importance of the learning environment in the professional development and training of teachers, as much as in the classroom with pupils and students.

Finally, it should be noted that, for some workshops, evaluative activities may be built into the workshop procedure itself. For example, the checklists in the "Initial reflections" section are, in themselves, evaluative – although the appropriateness of the processes used may still need to be assessed. In another workshop, "Race and racism", participants are asked specifically to identify and prioritise further areas for learning. In the "Policy development and review" section, the evaluative process appears as part of the final workshop, but it should be assumed that the 'process model' of policy development presented in this section should be assessed – and adjusted – so that it is relevant to each individual educational institution.

## EVALUATING THE WORKSHOPS            SAMPLE SHEET

··································································································

**WORKSHOP TITLE**

··································································································

**1** The purpose of the workshop is to:

**3** What issues raised in the workshop do you feel were most important?

How far do you think that these issues have been effectively addressed in this workshop?

**4** What issues raised in the workshop would you like to follow up, or find out more about?

**2** How useful and relevant were the support materials used in this workshop? Can you suggest any alternatives or improvements?

**5** Have you any other comments to make about:
- the style and presentation of the workshop?
- the domestice arrangements?
- any other issues?

# An annotated bibliography

**Note:** We make no claim that this bibliography is comprehensive, or even fully representative of publications in this field. What we have tried to do is draw together a select bibliography of materials which are relatively up-to-date and obtainable and which may be useful as background reading to many of the workshops in this manual. Further references, particularly to classroom materials, can be found in specific sections of the handbook which accompanies this volume, and in support of the discussion paper in Appendix 1.

Ashrif, S (1986) **Eurocentrism and Myopia in Science Teaching** in **Multicultural Teaching,** 5.1, Autumn. A relatively short article, but argues fiercely and cogently for an anti-racist approach which takes on board the historical contexts and contributions of black people to science. Packed full of examples. Later articles by Ashrif on anti-racist approaches to science are equally valuable but sadly not widely published at present.

Brandt, G. (1987) **The Realisation of Antiracist Teaching,** Falmer Press. An excellent book which made the first serious attempt to link antiracist 'theory' in education with classroom practice. Case studies, includes classroom practice in science and contains discussions on planning appropriate processes and contexts to promote equality.

Ditchfield, C. (compiler) (1987) **Better Science: Curriculum Guide 7; Working for a Multicultural Society,** Heinemann/ASE for the SCDC. A concise but comprehensive discussion of the field, moving into antiracist education. Very useful for a teacher wishing to survey the field or initiate developments in a school or department.

Egglestone et al. (1986) **Education for Some,** Trentham Books. Published shortly after the "Swann Report", the "Egglestone Report" delivers a strong edictment of the way in which black students are treated by schools – both in terms of their day-to-day experiences and their achievement and vocational destinations. A standard reference for discussing isses of race equality, a summary booklet is available from the Runneymede Trust.

Gill, B. (1989) **Indicators and Institutional Evaluation** in **Multicultural Teaching,** 8.1. Autumn 1989 Trentham Books, In this article the author discusses issues of managing and evaluating change in antiracist education. Represents an interesting contrast to more laissez-faire approaches to anti-racism and argues that 'success' does, indeed, need to be evaluated where race equality initiatives are concerned.

Gill, D and Levidow L (eds) (1987) **Anti-racist Science Teaching,** Free Association Books. A radical critique of science and science teaching which also includes some suggested curriculum approaches. Valuable on theoretical issues and provides some practical teaching strategies – although few chapters address issues in primary schools.

Gould, S.J. (1984) **The Mismeasure of Man**, Pelican. A detailed study of attempts by 19th Century scientists to place people into preconceived groups by scientific tests. An indictment of the misuse of intelligence testing.

Hollins, M (ed) (1984) and (1986) **Science Teaching in a Multiethnic Society**, Volumes 1 and 2, North London Science Centre. Volume 1 is an introductory booklet about the range of issues concerning science education, useful as a starter, despite being a little dated. Volume 2 contains a valuable collection of sources of material for teaching science. Particularly useful on historical aspects.

Hoyle, P (1987) **Issues in Science Education: Developing an Antiracist Approach**. An in-service discussion pack. Limited publication by the author. In some ways, a fore-runner of this manual. A useful resource for schools, departments, advisers and trainers.

Laine, C. and Hoyle P (1989) **Talking Science** HBJ Schools. As well as being a useful resource for the classroom, the teacher's book of this pack addresses a range of issues surrounding language development in science teaching, using practical examples to show how language can be developed, addressing the needs of bilingual learners, and how to incorporate anti-racist and anti-sexist approaches.

Nott, M and Watts, M (1987) **Education in Science**, April. A critique of the DES policy document "**Science 5-16: a statement of policy**". The authors suggest that the document falls short of grasping the nettle of multicultural education, let alone issues of racism.

Peacock, A (ed), 1991 **Science in Primary Schools: the Multicultural Dimension**, Macmillan. Right up-to-date and reflecting National Curriculum which many others listed, do not. Excellent articles on rationale and practice with plenty of practical classroom suggestions. Takes a broad view of the multicultural/anti-racist field.

Rattansi, P.M. (1985) **History and Philosophy of Science and Multicultural Science Teaching**, in G Brandt, A, Turner and S Turner **Science Education in a Multicultural Society** Report of a conference, University of London, Institute of Education. A provocative paper discussing the role of discovery learning in science education, reflecting on the implications this method of teaching might have for the stature of past scientists and peoples of different cultures.

## AN ANNOTATED BIBLIOGRAPHY                CONTINUED

Richardson, R. (1990) *Daring to be a Teacher*, Trentham Books. Not much about science but lots about teaching children! This should be compulsory reading for everyone involved in education. Richardson offers inspiration to his profession and reveals the real liberating spirit of education for equality and justice into the 1990s. Always entertaining and challenging: read this book whenever inspiration is needed!

Roach T., Smith, D. and Vasquez, M (1990) *Language and Learning in the National Curriculum: Bilingual Pupils and Secondary Science*, Hounslow Schools Language Centre. An excellent collection of resources for science teachers. It includes a valuable discussion of the role of language in learning and provides useful guidance for teachers who are developing teaching and learning materials in science for all pupils, not just developing bilinguals. An adapted version of this paper appears in the handbook.

Rose, S et al. (1985) *Not in our Genes: Biology, Ideology and Human Nature*, Pelican. A comprehensive and uncompromising indictment of the use of biology and psychology to define 'human nature' and intelligence, and how this leads to inequalities on grounds of 'race', gender, class, etc., justified by the work of 'determinist' and 'reductionist' scientists. Excellent and readable.

Selby, D. (ed) (1985) *Global Pi: World Studies* in *The Science and Maths Classroom World Studies Journal*, Vol 5 No 4. A range of articles providing perspectives and ideas for World Studies approaches to teaching science and maths. Many issues of contexts, content and teaching styles are raised, although not always in great depth.

Shan, S-J (1990) *Assessment by Monolingual Teachers of Developing Bilinguals at Key Stage 1* in *Multicultural Teaching,* Vol 9, No 1, Autumn. Building on a range of stimuli in the early years classroom, this article highlights some of the contemporary issues in assessment at key stage 1 and offers practical strategies for teachers trying to implement the National Curriculum.

Shiva, V (1989) *Staying Alive: Women, Equality and Development*, Zed Books. Dr Shiva is an eminent Indian physicist and philosopher and in this book shows how western concepts of science have been applied in India to the detriment of the environment and the people, particularly the women, who live in rural areas. Powerfully links ecological and feminist perspectives to science in a global context.

Smith, D. and Tomlinson S. (1989) *The School Effect* P.S.I. A comprehensive research project which presents evidence to show that the quality of education has a profound effect on the education of children, and in particular black pupils. 'Good' schools, which have high expectations of all pupils and clear equal opportunities policy and practice, will benefit black children in their achievement. A valuable contribution to the field.

Swann *et al* (1985) *Education for All?*, H.M.S.O., A daunting official report of 1000 plus pages, but which contains much that is valuable in terms of establishing the reality of educational experience for many minority ethnic pupils in British schools. Some of the appendices are particularly useful. Although criticised for its equivocal stance towards racism in education, this volume remains a touchstone for debate. For a good 'summary' see the Runneymede Trust version rather than Lord Swann's own watered-down booklet.

Thompson, B. (convenor) (1985) *Science Education for a Multicultural Society*, Leicester L.E.A. A resource for the classroom teacher beginning to tackle issues of cultural diversity in science with examples of classroom practice and resources. A little dated, but still useful for starting points.

van Sertima, I. (ed) (1986) *Blacks in Science – Ancient and Modern*, Transaction Books, USA. Becoming a standard reference in the field, this book provides evidence to explode the myth that Africans were primitive and non-technological peoples. Fascinating examples of ancient civilisations developing sophisticated science and technology are presented. Notes are also provided on more contemporary Black contributions to Science – mainly in the USA.

## THE WRITERS

### MEMBERS OF THE A.S.E. MULTICULTURAL EDUCATION WORKING PARTY

ANNA CHAPMAN is Coordinating Advisory Headteacher for Bilingualism in Oxfordshire.

FRANK CHENNELL is Advisory Teacher for Science Education in Norfolk.

CHRISTINE DITCHFIELD is Assistant Education Officer (Governor Services) in Cumbria.

CHRISTINE EDWARDS is Organiser of the 16+ programme in the INSET Division of Leeds University School of Education.

ESME GLAUERT is Primary Science Advisory Teacher in the London Borough of Hackney.

PAULINE HOYLE is Adviser for Science Education in the London Borough of Islington.

ALYSON JENKINS worked, until recently, for a development education centre, and is a teacher and INSET provider in Dyfed.

TREVOR ROACH is Teacher in Charge at the Royal Forest of Dean Environmental Studies Centre.

KABIR SHAIKH is Chair of the Working Party, and Chief Inspector in the London Borough of Ealing.

SHARAN-JEET SHAN is General Adviser for Assessment in Sandwell Borough.

STEVE THORP is Vice-Chair and Convenor of the Working Party, and is Advisory Teacher for Multicultural Education in Northamptonshire.

SHEILA TURNER is a Senior Lecturer in Education at the University of London, Institute of Education.

TONY TURNER is a Lecturer in the Science Education Department at the University of London, Institute of Education.

SUE WATTS is Deputy Headteacher of the Eylwin School in the London Borough of Southwark.

## THE EDITOR

Steve Thorp is Vice-Chair of the ASE Multicultural Education Working Party and works as Advisory Teacher for Multicultural Education in Northamptonshire. He has a general science degree from Newcastle University, and a PGCE from Liverpool University. He taught and studied in schools in Oxfordshire before being appointed to his present post. Steve has a young family and is active in his local community. He is involved with the Woodcraft Folk and is also currently a school governor and local District Councillor.

## ACKNOWLEDGEMENTS

The project has been made possible by the many colleagues who have supported and constructively criticised our work, attended symposia, bought discussion packs and so on. It would also not have happened without the ongoing advice and support of ASE Committee members and officers who have allowed their own perspectives to be challenged and have continued to be positive about all aspects of our work. The members of the Working Party themselves (past and present) have put in so much time and expertise over the two years and it is their work which forms the backbone of this publication. The editing stage was supported by a B.P.-funded Fellowship and my employers, Northamptonshire L.E.A., who allowed me to be seconded during the summer term 1991. Much of the work took place at weekends at the Comet Hotel, Hatfield where the staff made sure we were well fed and watered. Thanks go to all these.

More specific thanks are due to:
Cathy Wilson, whose quiet diplomacy and efficiency ensured that the project developed smoothly; John Avieson, Jane Hanrott, Mavis Wallace and others at the ASE.
David Playfoot and Martin Skelton from Fieldwork who put the package together and Alex Szyszkowski for the design; David Turner and Margaret Davison from Brackley Professional Development Centre, and Farzana Turner and Steve Harrison, General Education Inspectors in Northamptonshire, for their professional support.

Thanks finally to Mary and the girls – and to all our partners, families, flatmates, etc. who put up with the regular weekend trips to Hatfield, after not seeing us much anyway, during the frantic weeks and months of the last few years in education. Let us work, hope and/or pray for more caring, gentle times to come!

**Steve Thorp: November 1991**